CAN YOU PUT IT ON A T-SHIRT?

To Doreen Montgomery
literary agent extraordinary

CAN YOU PUT IT ON A T-SHIRT?

Communication Skills for the 1990s

Godfrey Howard

DAVID & CHARLES
Newton Abbot London

British Library Cataloguing in Publication Data

Howard, Godfrey
   Can you put it on a T-shirt?:
   communication skills for the 1990s
   1. Communication skills
   I. Title
   302.2

ISBN 0–7153–9377–4

Printed in Great Britain
by Billing & Sons of Worcester
for David & Charles plc
Brunel House Newton Abbot Devon

Contents

Introduction to the New Communication Skills

A survey by one of the high-geared head-hunting agencies shows that our ability to master communication skills is at the top of the list in deciding how successful we are in work and life. This book is structured as your personal course in the new skills of relating to people and presenting yourself as well as products, services, causes and ideas. These skills are the latest discoveries about the human factor in information technology and are taught on top-level management courses costing thousands of pounds and dollars.

Every aspect of our lives is touched by this new knowledge, since the quality of any relationship – professional, commercial, even relationships of love and affection – is almost entirely dependent upon the quality of the communication between the people involved.

Press-button communication is standard everywhere. Modems and multiplexers link computers instantly to screens in different locations anywhere in the world. Yet every day reveals that everything hangs on dealing with people: someone's response to what you are saying or writing will make or break a deal, someone's say-so decides what will happen next. This book takes you to the heart of personal and intimate interplay between one person and another, brings unconscious forces to the surface so you can use them to open up new channels of person-to-person communication.

You will be introduced to a significant new field of research into the emotional, mental and physical differences between women and men, for reactions between the sexes remain complex whether it's in the boardroom, in the office, in the workshop or in bed. The anthropologist, Margaret Mead, warned that 'every marriage has to be rethought'; and so do relationships when men and women work together. The new skills alert you to change in the 1990s.

Every variable is up for grabs . . . Today, loving change, tumult, even chaos is a prerequisite for survival, let alone success.

Tom Peters, *Thriving on Chaos*

Advertising is pushing back the frontiers of communication, promoting dynamic linguistic and visual innovation to get a message across successfully. In this book you come into contact with outstanding creative ideas and learn to use them as you go into the next day – to handle a meeting, an interview, a telephone call, writing a letter or a fax – so they deliver what you need.

Business, politics and most other human activities are competitive, and the heat is on to succeed. Unless we are mystics living in our own inner world of non-doing, we are called upon to make things happen, to get things done. There is a line to be drawn, and good communication starts with respect for the other person: we learn how to keep a balance between conflicting pressures in the push and shove of the world, a balance in a constant state of adjustment, when 'achievement where it counts most . . .', according to Mike Bett, vice-chairman of British Telecom, '. . . is bottom-line profitability'.

We start with an insight into the essence of communication, into what makes people react and respond in a positive way. And as you acquire this understanding, you are led into detailed know-how of the new communication skills. Every chapter ends with a *Review of Communication Skills*, skills you can put to use the very next day – which is important, for research into teaching methods shows time and time again that to make new knowledge part of us, we must *use* it as soon as possible. So you are asked to follow this simple programme:

Read each chapter at your own pace and use each *Review of Communication Skills* to fix in your mind what you have learned.

The *next day* practise some of the new techniques, new knowledge, new understanding you have read about. They will then become part of you and you will experience a new awareness of people and how to communicate with them.

In the fast lanes of the 1990s, the skills you learn in this book will transform your working life and enable you to react more positively, more quickly and more successfully.

1 The Primeval Miracle of Communication

How to switch on to people and pick up the flow of their reactions
How to make people want to talk to you and listen to you
How to keep someone's confidence when something goes wrong
How to know what to put into a letter and what to leave out
How to build good business and personal relationships

Communication is a strange thing. Michael Tippett, the London-born composer, marvelled at the way we receive a letter through the post – 'sheets of lines and blobs on paper', he said, and when we take it out of the envelope, we imagine we can hear 'the loved (or hated) voice speaking out of the ink'. He called it the 'primeval miracle of communication'.

The human psyche is a strange thing and defies ultimate analysis. So does communication. *The Concise Oxford Dictionary* sidesteps the mystery of defining it as 'the act of imparting', which is typical of the way writers of dictionaries explain the inexplicable.

The 'act of imparting' is supposed to cover anything from someone tapping you on the shoulder to attract your attention, to the marvel of Michelangelo's ceiling in the Sistine Chapel, to the mastery of a late Beethoven quartet, to lovers holding hands, to a frustrated lorry-driver winding down his window and shouting 'Fuck off!' In the complexities of the human situation, communication contributes most to our lives, one way or another; at the same time it is something we take most for granted.

Yet behavioural studies show we are spending more and more of our time in what is called the *communication process*; the latest study put it at 80% of our waking hours. How long will it take you to read this book? Depending upon how fast you read, it will be so many hours out of your life – but that time could bring many dividends because the more we wake up to the miracle of communication, the more we shall be alert to how we can use it effectively, in more ways than we could ever have imagined possible.

Take £10m spent on an advertising campaign. Suppose different words and ideas selling the same product, could make 50% more people read the advertisements, look at the posters or give attention to the commercials: the advertising campaign would be worth an extra £5m, a lot of money.

What is that to you? Suppose every time you write an important letter, send a fax that requires action, make a phone call to get something done or put something right, the effectiveness of that communication is stepped up by the same 50%. What would that do for you over a week, over a year, over ten years? How much more successful would you be? If you are in business for yourself, how much more would your profits increase? If you are working for a company, how much more would your salary go up? And 50% is only an example: a communication that uses the latest skills can be many times more successful.

How much do you think about communication, except for those times when you have to write a difficult letter or make a phone call that could bring about something you desperately want to happen? Faced with such demands, people rarely know how to go about it and the best they can do is look around for the 'right words'.

But if communication is primeval, why isn't it as instinctive and natural as breathing or walking? What is there to learn? The truth is we have all become so much more complex and involved in our reactions that new knowledge is required even about the most basic of human activities. One of the most humane of psychiatrists, Dr Jack Dominian, considers sex a '. . . marvellous means of communication with another person, a uniquely instinctive way of saying *thank you for being here*'. Yet so many people have doubts about it – even Germaine Greer admitted that she was 'always so concerned about whether we were doing it the right way'.

But now communication has superseded sex as the 'ever-interesting topic', because progress and profits depend upon it to such an extent. Communication, in this sense, is far more than passing on information: it is one mind interacting with another, and when that interaction is successful, powerful motivation and the right action follow. Words are nearly always involved, but some of the most dynamic new communication skills are non-verbal. We communicate by the way we enter a room, the way we lift our heads, the way we look across the table at someone else.

The so-called 'head-up device', or 'sincerity machine', was first used in Britain by President Reagan in his Westminster Hall speech . . . Mrs Thatcher took eagerly to the device, which enables her to turn her head from side to side to look at the whole of her audience.

Michael Cockerell, *The Listener*

Communication works as a synergism, with the combined effect of a number of things, some seemingly trivial, building up to a successful result. Important conferences are planned with meticulous detail so everything is geared to getting the right message across. Nothing is left out, even the colour of the curtains is carefully chosen, as there is evidence that lighter colours encourage a more relaxed mood and darker ones seem more determined and resolute.

Now for a statement so simple it is all too easy to nod your head in agreement and then forget it. In the stress of a difficult encounter or negotiation, it is hard to hold on to this principle, yet when you leave it out, you severely cut down your chance of success. Here it is: *Communication only exists in relation to someone else.* Otherwise we end up talking to ourselves, which is why most negotiations fail, even at the highest level of diplomacy.

The most advanced technology can put us almost instantly in touch with anyone, anywhere, from wherever we are, but it is only a tool for us to use. After we have pressed the button, we remain with the problems and perplexities of having to relate to someone else in a way that will lead to the result we want. We have to be as switched on as possible to the other person, whether they're at the end of a line on the other side of the world, or sitting facing us at the other side of our desk.

There are two easy techniques that are extraordinarily effective in helping us both to focus on another person or on a group of people we are in contact with, and to tune in to the flow of their reactions. To do this successfully will often make the difference between understanding and cooperation, or obstruction and a negative response. Similar techniques are taught to highly-paid executives on costly management courses and are used by people at the top in different fields in many countries.

The first technique makes use of our eye muscles. It is practised by some artists to help them relate more intensely to what they are looking at. Try this next time you are talking to someone, in person or on the telephone. Experiment with relaxing your eyeballs, especially the muscles that help the eyes to function – these muscles often become tense in moments of stress, yet to relax them is not nearly as difficult as it sounds: it's enough simply to become aware of your eyes in their sockets and relaxation usually follows. The effect is to release us momentarily from some of the subjectivity that hems us in, so that we are more receptive and responsive to the people or the situation confronting us.

The second technique, which is an alternative method, uses our breathing. It is an ancient yogic discipline that has been adapted as one of the skills in communication for the 1990s: all you do is allow yourself to become aware of your breathing. There is no need to breathe more deeply or more audibly, as that could be counterproductive. There is no need to change anything: it is enough simply to notice your normal inhalation and exhalation. If this seems to you too simple to make any difference, think back to the last time you were unable to do something until someone who had been there before pointed out what you had overlooked. And maybe you felt rather stupid at not having seen it for yourself!

Both these techniques heighten awareness of our surroundings and particularly of the people we are dealing with at that moment. They open up a wider channel of communication and break through what Tagore (who worked on these techniques for himself) called 'the invisible screen of the commonplace', so that our approach becomes livelier and more daring.

It is best to find out for yourself which of these two exercises suits you. It is important to try them both at different times and in different situations to see which comes more easily and more naturally. Some people switch from one to the other, some use them both at the same time; there is no rule, except to practise either one until it becomes part of the way you work.

Human beings are not two-dimensional, and the new skills in communication have dimensions beyond the ones we normally perceive. Aldous Huxley, who was deeply interested in parapsychology, said that most of us 'encapsulate ourselves', wrap ourselves round with myopic perceptions, which cuts us off from other people, even though we may *seem* friendly and outgoing.

Huxley wrote *The Doors of Perception* to describe his experience of enlarging consciousness through the use of mescalin and LSD. Such things may seem remote from our day-to-day work dealing with people and getting things done. But relaxing the eye muscles or making ourselves aware of our breathing follow the same path, although not to those dangerous extremes. They are tested and effective methods of opening our personal 'doors of perception'. Try using one of these techniques next time the chips are down and you are facing a tough negotiation or are at the wrong end of a difficult confrontation. It may help you to see a line of communication that will get round the problem.

You do not need to make a note of these techniques here and now: they are set out in the *Review of Communication Skills* at the end of the chapter.

If you had the opportunity to follow an executive through a day in their life – as an unseen witness – you would learn a great deal about skills in communication, both from good examples and perhaps even more from bad ones. Because it would not be your life but someone else's, you would be free from the anxiety of being involved and able to observe more clearly why some encounters succeed, and why others go badly wrong. Let us go on to share part of one particular day in the life of Anne Ridgeway, marketing manager of Oxford Plastics. Although a day in her life will not be the same as a day in yours, you will recognise familiar patterns and problems and will be able to take a fresh look at the next day ahead for you.

Anne is thirty-five, has fair hair and attractive blue eyes. She was one of the first women to take an MBA degree and lives with her boyfriend, Terence, in a flat in a converted period house in a square in Islington, now a fashionable district on the north side of central London. Her day begins early, as she expects to be at her desk in Oxford Plastics' offices on the edge of the City by 8 o'clock.

She gets up at 6.30am, or as near to that time as she can bear, depending on the evening before. Terence also has to leave early and they have an unsmiling uncommunicative breakfast together of toast and coffee. Anne is already thinking about the difficult problem she has to face that day. Besides the many other applications of plastic packaging, Oxford Plastics designs and manufactures plastic cosmetic pouches for Naturella Cosmetics. Today is D-day, the agreed delivery date of 250,000 packs, and they are not going to make it. Anne is leaning on the breakfast table, her head resting on her cupped hand, as she sips her coffee and mulls over the problem ahead.

A laconic 'Bye darling' follows, with a hurried habitual kiss, and she runs downstairs to get into her white automatic Honda coupé parked in the street outside. Unseen by her, we open the passenger door and slip into the seat beside her. We notice that Anne is a confident, assured driver; she joins the City-bound traffic, not too heavy as yet but already with an insistent throb, a warning of the rush-hour to come.

Anne has been up for less than an hour and already she has put up a major barrier to good communication. We all do it at times. Some people do it all the time and it always makes the contact with someone else ineffective and unsatisfactory. Instead of focussing on the here and now, on the person we are speaking to at that moment, our minds have gone ahead to grapple with the problem to come. Anne's ten-minute breakfast with Terence – the most important man in her life, she would say – might never have happened. If asked, she couldn't have told you what he was wearing: the contact between them was almost non-existent.

We have all been at the receiving end of this kind of switch-off, when the person we are talking to or appealing to, perhaps our doctor or our lawyer, is clearly in a hurry and preoccupied with something else. We leave frustrated and dissatisfied with the meeting.

Hurry is the enemy of proper doctoring, and all the great men I have known seem to have all the time in the world for patients or for their juniors and colleagues. The patient must feel you have nothing on your mind except his problem . . .

Dr David Mendel, *Proper Doctoring*

Let's hope there is enough reserve of love and goodwill between Terence and Anne for it not to matter so much, but if she carries over the same attitude to other encounters during the day, she will lose out.

The first rule of good communication with anyone is to be there, keeping your mind as free as you can from anything that does not relate to what you are saying or listening to at that moment. This doesn't come easily to begin with, but with practice you can make it a habit, a good habit that will make other people want to see you, talk to you and listen to you. Five minutes of that kind of attention from someone brings more results than an hour's dispersed discussion. Executives at the top usually have an uncluttered desk, and when you are talking to them, nothing else seems to get in the way. Even if you can't manage to focus your own attention to such a degree, at least come out from behind the clutter and sit with your back to it when you are talking to someone. The eye muscle and breathing exercises described earlier (see p16) are both designed to help you focus on the other person. Try them.

Meanwhile Anne is halfway to her office near the City. Oxford Plastics' factory is some sixty miles outside London, on an industrial estate near Oxford. The factory opens up at 7.30am and we listen to Anne speaking on her carphone to Bob Shields, the production manager. She has not stinted herself on high-tech equipment: her cellphone has a voice-control module. She presses the *call* button above the dashboard and a pleasant robotic voice informs her:

'Ready'

'Dial' she commands.

'Name?' it asks.

'Bob Shields'

The telephone number and name come up on a small screen.

'Please check' she is advised.

'OK!'

'Dialling. . .'

Bob Shields answers.

So far so good. Technology has done its work and has already put her in touch with the problem of dealing with Naturella Cosmetics' order, while she is negotiating the traffic on the way to the office. How is she dealing with it?

Anne: 'Surely you must have known that you were going to be late with this order. Why didn't you warn me so that I could have taken it up with the customer?'

Bob Shields is on the defensive. He knows from experience that Anne can be assertive and make him feel small. Maybe it's because she's a woman, he thinks, and has to prove something. He explains to her that in the middle of the job the oscillator had blown on the high-frequency welder.

Anne: 'What kind of a shop are you running there? Don't you carry spares?'

'It's not as easy as that.' Bob tells her. He reminds her that oscillators are costly, and since they have a shelf life of less than a month, to keep valid spares all the time would be wasteful. By now, Anne is swinging her Honda into the car park.

'I'll call you back from the office,' she says and cuts off. As she parks her car and goes up to the office, she has a griping feeling that she's not getting anywhere. And she's right.

Effective communication always starts with the question: *What do I want to achieve?* It focusses on what has to be done, not on what has gone wrong. It is a misplaced priority to hold an inquest while the patient is still alive. An examination of what has gone wrong does have an important place, of course, to find out ways to prevent a recurrence. But all that should be deferred so that nothing gets in the way of dealing with the immediate problem.

Anne does better when she calls Bob Shields back and we listen to her focussing directly on the problem in hand: 'How many of the packs were finished before the oscillator went on you?'

Bob goes away to check and comes back with the answer: 'About 50,000.'

Anne: 'That's a fifth of the order. Not much maybe, but it's something to offer. How soon can you get them ready for despatch?'

He talks about the next day, because they have to be inspected, packed and so on. Anne brings it forward to later that same afternoon. As we are listening, we admire the way she smoothes out the bristling resentment she had aroused in the production manager by her earlier conversation with him. She started off on the wrong foot but is putting it right as soon as she can, not by backing down or being conciliatory, but by showing she understands what has happened. She tells him what she is going to say to the customer and ends the call:

'Brilliant! I hope the day goes well for you. And let me know right away if there's anything we can do this end.'

She knows it's not likely they can do anything from the London office, but she leaves Bob Shields feeling he is supported and that she knows how to deal with the problem from her end.

If people can see you know your job . . . that you communicate with them and tell them what you're doing . . . they will respect you and they will work well for you.

Sir Hector Laing, chairman of United Biscuits,
Advice From The Top

For a few moments Anne looks out of the window at the criss-crossing traffic in the street below. She decides to send a fax to Graham Berman, the buyer at Naturella Cosmetics, to break the news to him. She thought she'd begin something like this:

We're despatching 50,000 gift packs to you direct from the factory this afternoon. These have come out well and I hope you're pleased with them . . .

Then she would go on to explain why the rest of the order was going to be late. She reaches for her fax pad – but shakes her head. That's not the way. She takes a deep breath and touches the automatic call button on her phone for Naturella Cosmetics.

She was right to change her mind. If there's something difficult to say, it's a great temptation to shelter behind a fax or a letter. But you are more likely to keep someone's goodwill by speaking directly to them as it gives them a chance to react, to let off steam, to ask questions. And it gives you a chance to respond in the most sensitive and reassuring way you can: 'I'm sorry', said in the right tone of voice, can sometimes make all the difference. There's no 'tone of voice' in a fax.

When Anne hangs up after speaking to Graham Berman, she reaches for her fax pad more confidently and writes out by hand a brief note confirming the essential points of her phone conversation. This is one of the best uses of a fax, to confirm a telephone call while it's still resonating in the other person's head. If it's a customer, it reinforces confidence; if it's a supplier, it underlines what is important to you. And if you write it by hand, as Anne does, it keeps up the person-to-person contact.

Unseen by her, we look over Anne's shoulder and see her add an afterthought at the end of her fax to Graham Berman:

Thank you for being so understanding. I do appreciate it.

Maybe that wouldn't sound right coming from a man, but coming from Anne it seems to strike a good note. She is far too competent to use being an attractive woman to cover up inadequacies. But she *is* a woman and is able to make contact with the warmth of feeling that flows naturally from her.

It's now 10 o'clock and time to say goodbye to Anne. What we have learned in the three hours we have been by her side will come up again in the *Review of Communication Skills* on p24.

Every communication, like every work of art, is selective. As in everything else in life, some things are more important than others; the trick is knowing which ones they are, and it is astonishing how often this is overlooked in reports, letters, speeches, sales pitches and telephone calls. It's an understandable temptation to put everything in the shop window in the hope that a passer-by will see at least one thing to attract them. That's all right in a bargain basement but it's not the best way to go about presenting a serious argument or proposal.

Whatever medium you are using for communication, what

you select to say or demonstrate can change the whole impact. In communication there is always a choice to be made, not only about what to include or what to leave out, but in the order you present things. These decisions can turn everything upside down for you if you get them wrong, and can change altogether what people think. Margaret Thatcher rightly complains that television is selective: she recalled opening a fine new hospital, but 'the only coverage was a demonstration outside – about cuts!'

How do you know what to put in and what to leave out? You look at it from the other person's point of view and ask yourself what are the things that matter to *them*. Every good copywriter works in this way and millions of pounds, dollars, pfennigs, francs, yen and so on are spent on research to find out what people really want. If we get that wrong, we're lost: when we get it right, we beat the competition.

The answers that always come near the top of the list – whatever the product, whatever the situation and wherever it is happening – are *reliability* and *service*, the confidence that nothing is likely to go wrong and the security of knowing that if it does, it will be put right with ungrudging willingness. If you are in business and you keep these two principles to the forefront, you might make a fortune. Your goods or service may cost more, because reliability and first-class service do not come cheap, but many of the most successful products in the world are not the cheapest on the market. One study reports that 'it costs five times more to go out and get a new customer than it costs to maintain a customer you already have'.

Anne Ridgeway understands this principle. We have seen how she ended her fax to her customer, Graham Berman. This is how she began it:

> I'm sorry something has gone wrong. But that must be our headache and not yours, because it's our job to put it right. You will get 50,000 packs this afternoon and the rest of your order will be delivered in seven days, come what may, even if we lose money on the job. And the quality will be what you want and expect.

As long as we have respect for the other person, we are not likely to go wrong over this. Respect for the other person is not a pious holier-than-thou precept, it is a reliable guide to how to conduct a relationship, whether in business or in the family. One of the art directors in the advertising agency, Ogilvy and Mather, has a notice over his drawing-board that constantly reminds him to treat readers of advertisements with respect:

THE CONSUMER IS DAVID OGILVY'S WIFE

Just in case you don't know, David Ogilvy is president of the agency.

It is rare for a shop selling clothes not to have a fitting-room where you can try them on. Some Marks and Spencer stores do not; but what every one of their stores *does* have is a customer service counter, where you can take anything back even if you bought it at another branch, without embarrassment or argument, and get a full cash refund. Surveys show that *St Michael* is the best loved brand name in Britain; few other shops are respected and trusted by their customers as much, because few other stores respect their customers as much.

You do not have to be selling goods or services to put this idea to work: it can contribute to every conversation you have, every phone call you make, every letter you write. It will pay long-term dividends, as it always has done, and will resolve many problems of communication. This book aims to live up to this: when you bought or borrowed it, the writer and the publisher became committed to you, committed to increasing your powers and understanding of communication, to opening up the way to new ideas. We believe this chapter has begun to do that and in the chapters that follow we shall go on doing our best to deliver the best goods on offer – in the business of communication.

REVIEW OF COMMUNICATION SKILLS

1. Use the two techniques described in this chapter to help you communicate effectively with another person or group of people, to make you more receptive to them, more successful at negotiations and quicker off the mark in dealing with reactions:

- Relax your eyeballs, especially the muscles that help the eyes to function. Begin by becoming aware of the eyes in their sockets and relaxation will follow.

- Allow yourself to become aware of your inhalation and exhalation, without changing the rhythm or depth of your breathing.

Try these out at meetings or one-to-one discussions or even on the telephone. Find out which technique works better for you and stay with that one, practising it from time to time until you slip into it automatically whenever you need it. Both techniques have been proved remarkably effective: if you practise them properly they will work for you.

2. The next time you speak to someone or to a group of people, try putting everything else out of your mind, especially the things you have to deal with next. Simply focus on what you are saying and who you are saying it to. This quality of attention gives other people more confidence in your authority and your ability.

3. When you communicate about something that has gone wrong, give *first* priority to putting it right. Leave out *why* it has gone wrong until afterwards, so that nothing comes between you and dealing with the immediate problem.

When you are dealing with a complaint give *minimum* time to explaining why things went wrong and *maximum* time to what you are going to do to put them right.

4. In putting over an idea, selling a product or a service, or trying to convince someone you are the right person for the job, give the highest priority to projecting *reliability* and *follow-up service*. Surveys continually show these are the two things most people care about most.

5. Always keep in mind that good communication starts with respect for the other person.

6. Use a fax to confirm a conversation while it is still fresh in the other person's mind. This can reinforce a customer's confidence or underline for a supplier what is important to you.

7. Write down straightaway one specific opportunity you expect to come up tomorrow when you can use a new technique, a new piece of knowledge, a new understanding you have read about in this chapter.

2 Marketing Yourself

How to be your own image-consultant
How to make your office or your desk give a positive impression
How to relate to changes in the 1990s
How to target the people who should know about you
How to get the right message across – about yourself

The analysis by professionals of the stressful and subtle business of marketing ourselves has revealed a whole series of new communication skills. Many people dislike the idea of 'selling themselves', although it is partly a matter of words because most of us find it perfectly acceptable to try to 'make a good impression'. We know from our own responses that the first impression someone or something makes can move us towards them or away. In fact, one of the leading image-consultants is called *First Impressions*.

The latest survey of job interviews shows that if we start off on the wrong foot, an opportunity may be lost forever: we are told that most interviewers make up their minds about candidates within the first few minutes of meeting them and it takes a lot to move them away from that first point of view. Everything about us communicates something about us. The clothes we wear, the cars we drive, the way we enter a room, even the way we sit down. Is the best message coming across for you, or are you unconsciously holding yourself back? You may not like thinking about this but it is as much a part of communication with other people as the words you use. Doctors no longer talk about a 'bedside manner' but the reality remains. It doesn't describe an ingratiating manner but the ability to reassure patients, which is the first step to helping them get better.

There's no need to be self-conscious about role-playing or creating an effect; people will see through that soon enough. But an intelligent appraisal of the ways your mental attitude and personal style will make other people react can often make the difference between convincing them or leaving them shaking their heads.

Suppose you had arranged to see the director in charge of your department, to talk about an increase in salary. You open the door of their office and wait hesitantly.

'Come in, John, and sit down' you are invited. You go in almost reluctantly, sit halfway forward on the chair, cross your legs and fold your arms. The director looks at you in a friendly way.

'What can I do for you?'

So far you have come across as indecisive and defensive, as someone who expects to be refused – the other person is calling all the shots. This may not be your style, but do you know what *your* style is? Make a point of observing yourself carefully as you go into a meeting or when you see a customer or someone else about something important to you. Observe yourself critically the way a producer watches an actor making an entrance: you will learn a great deal, which you can use to help yourself.

Just as a product is packaged for the marketplace, it is accepted in the 1990s that we have to think about our own packaging. We cannot help having an image, because no-one can be neutral. What we seem like to other people – the way we look, the way we move, smile, sit down on a chair – is all part of our image, part of our own personal marketing. And when you begin to work on it, all kinds of things change for you. We could argue that this isn't fair, as only our real abilities should determine our success. But think back to the last time you were shopping for anything in another country: the brand names are unfamiliar, so you look at what's on offer and choose a package that attracts you. In the same way, our own ability to give people confidence in us helps us to get the best from them and for them.

Even at the top, personal packaging has become vital. Prince Charles's image was so lack-lustre that his private secretary, now Sir David Checketts, brought in leading American PR consultants, Neilson McCarthy, to give the prince credibility as a future king. Image-consultants in Britain and the States can charge up to £1,000 or $2,000 for a one-to-one session, a personal appraisal of how you come across and what changes you should make in your personal presentation. Possibly some of it goes too far and image-consultants claim too much; but some of their recommendations work and can change many things for us. The insights you can gain from this chapter derive from consultations with psychologists and others who have studied all the facets of self-presentation, and with them you can do a lot for yourself. Let's see how you can go to work on marketing yourself more successfully – and look upon it not with anxiety or suspicion, but as a fascinating voyage of discovery.

An American study, the result of three years' research by the Center for Creative Leadership, implies that *more* attention to image is vital – particularly for women wanting to crack through the 'glass ceiling' that keeps them from reaching the top.

Victoria McKee, *The Sunday Times*

If we have exceptional talent or ability or drive, if we are a Mozart, a Brunel, an Olivier, a Terence Conran, a Laura Ashley, we are likely to make our mark whatever impression we give to others. These people are powerful and rare exceptions and nothing would have held them back for long. For the rest of us, the image we present will play a significant and at times a decisive part in how effective, and how successful we are.

If you saw that historic confrontation in 1961 between John Kennedy and Richard Nixon, you would never forget how much someone's image can swing a decision one way or the other. Listeners who heard that debate on radio had no doubt that Nixon had won – his arguments seemed compelling and his views on foreign policy clear-sighted. But for the many more millions who watched it on television, Kennedy stole the show. Nixon had not been well and looked tense and pale – apart from a '7 o'clock shadow', a slightly unshaven look – whereas Kennedy had just come in from campaigning in California and looked fit, vital and sun-tanned. As a result, that debate opened the doors of the White House to John Kennedy, and Richard Nixon had to wait another eight years before he could move in.

Television has changed the political scene more than any other factor. Leaders have to present themselves in person to be judged by the electorate who are, in effect, the customers who are going to buy, or not buy, the product offered. We may not want to buff up our image the way politicians do but we can learn some things from them, without surrendering personal integrity and style. Harold Macmillan was a nervous man by all accounts, yet he turned into 'unflappable Mac' as he learned to use television to become better known and better liked – he was one of the first in Britain to do this. His official biographer, Alastair Horne, recollects that: 'The schoolmasterly glasses disappeared, the disorderly moustache has been rigorously pruned, the smile is no longer toothy and half apologetic, and he is wearing a spruce new suit.'

Nor did Margaret Thatcher, down to earth and independent though she is, disdain such trivialities: she allowed her hairstyle to be changed, her teeth to be capped, and her voice to be lowered after lessons from an actor from the National Theatre. Image can be deadly and defeating if you don't watch out. In the early days of his presidential campaign, George Bush was losing the female vote because, it is said, he reminded too many women of their first husband. He worked hard to change that – and succeeded.

'What has all this to do with me?' you may ask. 'Who wants to take up residence at 10 Downing Street or in the White House?' That may not be your dream, but you may want to build up your own business or advance your career with a multinational company or achieve something else that requires other people to feel the right way about you. We all know that to succeed you have to work hard and push your abilities to their limits. But you also have to work at having the right effect on the people working for you, and on people whose decisions could change the pattern of your future.

Some of the most successful companies in the world – names such as IBM, Shell, Marks and Spencer – have seen the commercial value of hiring the skills of image-consultants to help their senior staff. Even holy writ has become aware of the importance of presentation in the 1990s: a publisher tells us 'It's just called 'The Bible' now – we dropped the word

'Holy' to give it a more mass-market appeal'. So the words we choose or leave out are an important part of marketing and can change people's attitude towards us. A survey commissioned for Price Waterhouse came up with the astonishing result that *job title* comes first as an incentive to applicants, even before salary and location.

It is good advice to look at the way marketing professionals are using words to see which way the wind is blowing. If you want to be in touch, you have to relate to changes in attitudes and to associations in people's minds. Car manufacturers are building on the response to the adventure of high-tech and space travel by talking about the driver's 'cabin', about modules, podules and instrument panels. SAAB takes the idea all the way by showing the SAAB *Carlsson*, named after the legendary rally driver, on a runway alongside the latest jet, declaring that from 0–60mph there is nothing much between them.

Apart from the products it sells, the books it publishes, the services it provides, the actual *name* of a company can have its own image by association – we might think of it as stuffy or lively, cautious or progressive, dull and routine, or exciting and innovative. And the difference can have a significant effect, one way or the other, on the value of a company's shares on the stockmarket, just as what people *think* about a man or a woman can have a significant effect on their value in an organisation. Martin Sorrell, whose WPP communications group has made brilliant takeovers, puts a direct financial value on the *name* of an advertising agency he is bidding for: 'Advertising agencies can be brands in the same way as "KitKat" or "Polo".'

Few of us want that level of brand-imagery for ourselves, but it can be useful for a moment to think of yourself as a brand name. Everything you do in your work, every memo or letter you write, every discussion you have plays a part in giving your 'brand name' an image and a value. This is a tough concept to live up to, as it demands that we keep in mind all the time that whatever we put our name to, through what we say or write or do, communicates something about ourselves, adds value to or takes value from our personal 'brand name'.

An essential part of marketing is getting known, because unless a product is on display in the shop window or on the counter inside, no-one is going to buy it. When contracts are made with leading actors they specify how big their names should be on the billboards, and who should come first; public relations companies eagerly tell their clients how many 'column inches' they have succeeded in getting for them in newspapers and magazines; academics stay up late writing articles for learned journals so their names can appear; *Ford* pays a small fortune for the privilege of sewing their logo on just *one* sleeve of Boris Becker's tennis shirt.

Does this have much to do with us, unless we work for Coca-Cola, Nescafé, Philips, Volkswagen, or any other company with a famous brand name? Yes, it has an important message: the constant reminder of the huge financial value of being known.

Individuals will not succeed unless top management know of their existence, their desires and ambitions. People who do not get noticed get overlooked and left behind.

John Holmes, chairman of Holmes & Marchant

In corporate life we have to see the importance of standing out from the crowd, of somehow keeping ourselves out in front. This is true if you are starting your own business, taking your first job straight from college, if you want to get into local politics, or get a chair at Oxford or Yale in ancient history. The people who can help you have to know about you.

Unless we are a brand name or a star, we don't need to get known by millions – we have the advantage of being able to target the people who matter to us. Start off by making a list of the people who need to be reminded of your existence and of what you have to offer them – it may be only a dozen or so, or it may be every woman between eighteen and fifty living within five miles of your hairdressing salon. Or it could be every company in town that might need a high-speed fax translation service.

Defining your target audience as accurately as possible takes time and research, but every hour, every pound, every dollar you spend on it will be repaid countless times over. Targeting comes into more than one chapter of this book because one of the most effective power skills is aiming a communication at the right person or people in a particular situation. You have to work at identifying whose are the say-sos that really count.

You will have picked up by now that the communication

process of marketing yourself is not far removed from marketing a brand name or a company. As with a product on the shelf, it is not only *who* you are but *how you look* to other people. British Petroleum recently spent a million pounds – about 2 million dollars – on research and design of the letters *BP* for their new logo, the aim being to achieve a 'fresh new identity for the 1990s'. They considered it worth spending a lot of money on what they *look* like.

Design consultancy has become one of the fastest growing service industries in industrialised countries. Companies are facing up to the way they look to the outside world because they now realise it could have a decisive effect on how customers, their own employees and their shareholders support them. It's not so very different when it comes to individuals: we are all dependent upon how others relate to us.

One of the most significant reasons why people do not advance is because of their personal style and its effect on others.

Paul Massey, vice-president,
Institute of Personnel Management

Design is an integral part of personal communication: the clothes you wear, the way your office or your desk looks, the way you present a letter, a fax or a report all say something about you. A letter starts to communicate even before we read it: the layout, paper, heading make the first impression. The company sending it might be no more than one person working from home but it can still carry an image of substance and reliability. When Maurice Saatchi wanted the Saatchi & Saatchi agency to break away from the feeling that ad agencies were not sound vehicles for financial investment, he briefed the designer of their notepaper to *make us look like a bank*.

The Department of Trade and Industry in Britain places such a high importance on right design that it launched a campaign of whole-page advertisements in newspapers, using headlines such as:

Don't let poor design endanger
your livelihood

That is directed at manufacturing and service businesses, but we could also say:

Don't let poor design endanger
your career

If we believe in marketing ourselves, we must do what every business should do, from the shop around the corner to a multinational: review our decisions and indecisions about design. We are advised by some consultants to walk into our office – the room we normally take for granted – or to look at our desk, as if we had never seen it before. Then ask: *What does it tell you about the person using it?* The higher people go in authority and responsibility, the less you usually see on their desks. Some chief executives don't even have a desk, as presumably they deal with everything as soon as it comes in.

David Ogilvy, who invented almost single-handed the concept of image, offers more guidelines about the impact of the design of our offices:

If they are decorated in bad taste, we are yahoos. If they look old-fashioned, we are fuddy-duddies. If they are too prestigious, we are stuffed shirts. If they are untidy, we look inefficient.

Decide what you want to communicate, and then make whatever changes are necessary and possible to your office and your desk – with effort and imagination you can usually make more changes than you think are possible.

Some courses on personal presentation advise us to take all our clothes out of the wardrobe and hang them around the room to see what image they project. We are told that Marilyn Monroe never wore the same dress twice and that Woody Allen always wears the same tartan shirt. Both approaches project an image, although one costs a great deal more! There is no doubt that clothes present a more difficult problem for women in business than for men, because women's clothes are less regulated and have a much greater potential for projecting sexuality.

In design, imagination and flair ride high. An executive in an investment company on Park Avenue spends as little as he can on suits and as much as he can on shirts and ties – the effect is to make him look expensively dressed! The head of a French marketing company follows a similar line by always wearing ordinary plain dresses, enhanced by the most exquisite and expensive Florentine leather belts.

The tendency is for most highly-paid Euro-managers to be unobtrusively dressed, but in the best designer clothes, from a Burberry trenchcoat, an Italian lightweight suit down to their Gucci shoes. One experienced consultant advises that we should first of all list the personal qualities we have and which we need to project, and then look for ways of expressing those qualities in what we wear. Politicians and company spokesmen appearing on television get expert guidance on what to wear and how to look to convey the impression they want. And it's not so very different for any one of us, whether we're going into a meeting, calling on a customer or being interviewed.

Some experts tell us that dark suits and plain or discreetly striped shirts give an impression of serious intent, while light-coloured suits and check shirts convey a relaxed attitude and innovative talent. Although proof of this kind of thing can never be conclusive, there is some evidence to support the suggestion. So if you are a financial adviser on the one hand, or a design consultant on the other, perhaps you should consider whether there is anything in all this for you, if it is not reflected already by your own personal style.

A company communicates with us the moment we enter its offices. Even the most out-of-touch chairmen have come to realise that very often the first employee a visitor encounters is the receptionist – even a visitor at the highest level. In the 1990s you are more likely to see that front-of-house position occupied by an attractive woman who looks up at you with real interest and sells you on the business right from the beginning, by her style, her manner and her knowledge of the people in the company. When he was chairman of ICI, John Harvey-Jones recalls that even the butler in the VIPs' dining-room '. . . recognises he represents ICI, and that he gives a whole series of messages to others about the company, its people, the sort of business it runs, and its behaviour and its expectations of behaviour'. Even if you don't have a butler or your own personal receptionist, you may have a secretary or an assistant or an answering machine. And the impression they make will rub off on to you and your image: they are part of the way *you* communicate.

Christopher Lawson became one of the first directors of

marketing for a political party in Britain, when he was taken on by the Conservative Party. He was called 'the man from Mars' because he had moved across from being a director of the company that makes Mars Bars. When he was asked about marketing and how it works for people as well as for products, his reply is worth recording: 'It's communication. It's getting the message across.'

How can you apply that to yourself? What do you sound like, for example, when you talk at meetings or on the telephone? The only way to find out is to listen to yourself, because the way you use your voice has a considerable effect on others – though when people talk about someone's voice, they often mean the mood that voice conveys. In fact it is very hard work to change your voice, although this can be done with professional help. But it's not so difficult to change the mood behind it: just speaking more slowly can make us seem more confident. Eliminating 'ers' and 'ums' will make us sound less doubtful; and making sure we don't say 'but' too often will help us appear less stick-in-the-mud. From time to time *listen* to how you use your voice: try it for a short period every day. But here is a warning: the experience may be painful. It will also be rewarding, as you will hear things you want to change – and can change without much effort. In particular, listen for the *energy* in your voice because that contributes so much to how convincing you sound.

We also communicate by the expressions on our face, and by the way we move. So it is not by chance that when you see President Bush on television, you see him looking fit and athletic, walking briskly or running up the gangway into the presidential aircraft: people are known to associate the leader's state of health with the health of the nation.

Bush . . . has released for publication the results of his most recent rectal examination . . . The American public needs to be reassured that the country will be governed for another four years by a healthy asshole.
Stephen Greenblatt, *London Review of Books*

And in November 1990, when Margaret Thatcher faced a

daunting challenge from Michael Heseltine, for the leadership of the country, she continued to walk confidently and purposefully into 10 Downing Street right up to the end. She had learnt to smile, even when the chips were down and she had to resign.

Smiling is important; it helps us to look in control of the day – if we appear downcast and disappointed, we look as if we're on the run. But remember that forced smiles look agonised. A trick that television presenters use in order to smile at will is to recall some episode or story that made them laugh spontaneously – for most of us, that will also bring on a smile! Try it next time you have to look cheerful in the face of adversity. It does work and is often used as a situation-saving lifeline by people who have to be prepared at any time to face an audience or television cameras.

The total impression of yourself as you appear to other people is built up from a number of small, seemingly insignificant things, just as a painting comes together from an innumerable number of brush strokes. It is not a matter of 'putting on an act'. People really do need to know about you if you are to advance in your work and develop your business or professional interests. It is up to you to make sure they get the right information. Remember what 'the man from Mars' said about self-presentation:

It's communication. It's getting the message across.

REVIEW OF COMMUNICATION SKILLS

1. Marketing yourself starts with observing yourself, just as marketing a product or a service starts with an appraisal of what the product or service looks like and the impact it makes on the people *who would buy it*.

Observe yourself entering a room to talk to someone. Afterwards write down what you noticed and anything you want to change. This is one of those simple exercises that, properly carried out, can tell you as much about yourself as an expensive session with an image-consultant.

2. Think of yourself as a *brand name*, a product in the marketplace. As you go through a working day, take into account that everything you do, say and write adds value to or takes value from your 'brand image'.

3. Make a list of the people or categories of people who need to know about you in order for the profitability of your business to increase, or for you to take the next step up in your career. Remember how much it costs Ford to sew their logo on just *one* sleeve of Boris Becker's tennis shirt! Ford can afford to spread its shots wide: for most of us *accurate* targeting is a vital skill. Give it all the time you can.

4. Whenever you can, use *good design* to present to the world the image that will do the most for you. It may be your notepaper, the way you present a report, how you make a fax look, the design of your shop, your factory, your office or just the way you arrange your desk.

5. Before you leave for work tomorrow morning, look in a full-length mirror and ask what your clothes tell other people about you. Then decide whether you want to do anything about it, even if only to buy a *couturier* tie or a beautiful leather belt from Florence!

6. Encourage everyone who works for you, or represents you in any way, to give to others the impression that you would want to give yourself. Never take this for granted – check this image-projection regularly.

7. Make a point of *listening* to your voice for a few minutes every day. Listen to the mood it conveys, and if there are things you want to change, work on them. If necessary get professional help, because your voice can be as important as the way you look.

8. Learn to smile even when the going is rough. It helps to tell people you are on top of the situation. A good technique, often used by television presenters, is to flash into your mind some episode or remark that made you laugh spontaneously: the spark jumps across and you find yourself smiling.

9. Write down straightaway one specific opportunity you expect to come up tomorrow when you can use a new technique, a new piece of knowledge, a new understanding you have read about in this chapter.

3 Don't Join the Queue

How to make people listen to you and read what you've written
How to come up with original ideas
How to involve people right from your first sentence
How to write reports people actually read
How to make figures and statistics 'sit up and talk'

You are sitting down with a blank sheet of A4 paper in front of you, trying to find the right words for a whole-page advertisement in a major newspaper. The advertising space costs £30k, to use the in-touch way of writing £30,000 – about $60,000. And now wait for the crunch: *you* are going to pay for it!

If you could get into that frame of mind before writing an important letter or making an important telephone call or drafting a report a lot hangs on, certainly it would add to the stress, but it would screw up your imagination and concentration to their highest possible pitch. And that leads to outstanding communication.

As you are writing the advertisement, aware of the price tag on the space, the first thing to frighten you would be that not enough people would look at it, let alone read it. You know only too well that the ever-mounting volume of messages competing for everyone's attention is so high now, that if your advertisement is to be worth the money, it must be out of the ordinary, it must make us want to look at it and look again. Otherwise it will simply join the queue, and if that happens, it's hit and miss whether anyone will get round to reading it. What a waste of money and energy that would be. Your money! Your energy!

In the heat and dust of an advertising agency you learn soon enough that advertising is not just a message from someone who has something to say to someone who is waiting to listen. Every advertisement has to fight like fury for attention since it must compete with all the other advertisements, posters, pretty women, attractive men and the multitudinous images that pass across our retinas, as well as all the other ideas and thoughts that clutter up our minds.

In some way, all our communications – letters, faxes, conversations – are up against that kind of competition. Don't lose heart because you will learn skills in this chapter to help you rise above the general level of the mass – or morass – of communications, to give yourself a better chance of being read and listened to. But we should never forget the competition, unless we want our communication – whatever its form – to join the queue.

Even when a letter is addressed to someone, they are not sitting there waiting to give it their undivided attention . . . unless it's a letter between lovers. Next time there's a stack of mail waiting for you and you start going through it, notice how quickly you put some letters on one side and focus more intently on others. Some things catch our interest and imagination, while others go into the 'pending tray' of our minds.

A most unlikely marketing genius, an American railway clerk named Richard Sears, invented selling by post. About a century ago, in 1891, he set out as an essay in moonlighting, to sell watches by writing to people about them. The floodgates opened, and before long the Sears and Roebuck catalogue, a thousand pages thick, was selling almost anything you could think of by post – ploughs, printing-presses and cure-alls, as well as watches, of course. The bandwagon has never stopped, and in the 1990s the direct-mail industry has become the fastest growing form of sales promotion in the world.

In Britain alone, direct-mail selling has trebled in value since the mid-1970s so that it now accounts for over 18% of all advertising expenditure. Daily post bags are ever more cluttered and the pressure increases all the time for advertisers to find new ways to make people stop and look. If your work involves communication – and whose doesn't? – that's the business you are in, too. We live in an age of communication when more and more information is being pumped into one ear and flows straightaway out of the other, very often without affecting us or motivating us.

Is Anyone Taking Any Notice? is the urgent title of a book of photographs by Donald McCullin, an internationally famous war photographer, born of a poor family in a north London tenement slum. He travelled all over the world, recording war, hunger, disasters and catastrophe: a woman lost and drifting in Mother Theresa's House of Dying in Calcutta, an American black hurling a live grenade in Vietnam, a gang of children on the rampage in Londonderry. The title of his book is an anguished cry from the heart, one we must remember every time we use words to help someone, or for a cause we care about, or for the good of our country, or the good of humankind. People turn away so quickly and words as Alexander Solzhenitsyn said in his speech accepting the Nobel Prize, 'run away like water, without taste, colour, smell'.

For a disquieting moment or two we have turned away from that blank sheet of A4 paper in front of us. But the point has been made: whether we are communicating for commercial or humanitarian reasons, an advertisement, a letter, even an important phone call needs something unexpected that will catch someone's attention, so that our message does not merge unnoticed into the background. Sometimes it can be what we have to offer that is exciting and different although more often it's not what we say but the way we say it. Charles Chaplin once claimed, 'All I need to make a comedy is a park, a policeman and a pretty girl'. He should have added, of course, 'plus the magic of genius', or at least a good idea, because the right idea transforms the most ordinary of things and makes it stand out from the crowd.

How do you value the punchline in an ad, when it could have been thought up in the bath . . . You have to measure genius as well as time. I'd love to be able to develop a formula for that.

Alicja Lesniak, financial director,
J Walter Thompson Group UK

Michael Tippett, the composer who gave us the title of the second chapter of this book, said about the Beatles, 'Their unique quality was to know at which points a scrap of ordinary language needed to be touched to make it sing'. Staying with music for another beat, great orchestras need marketing directors now, as well as musical directors. Judy Graham does that job for the London Philharmonic and she hired Saatchi & Saatchi to give the orchestra more popular appeal. As part of their first advertising campaign, they came up with a cheeky poster: it was Mike Hecht, the orchestra's principal trombonist, *almost* kissing his wife. The headline:

ANY CLOSER AND THE TROMBONIST COULD LOSE CONTROL

It was a small poster, but we looked at it – and looked again. The wit and humanity of the idea hooked our attention and it was good for the London Philharmonic Orchestra.

Not many of us have the job of promoting the brass section of a famous orchestra but most of us sometime or another have to write an application for a job, or help someone else write one. David Ogilvy, the most famous adman of our time, put being different almost at the top of the list for successful communication. When he started his own ad agency in New York, in 1948, he believed his English accent gave him a 'terrific advantage' because it set him apart from all the other ad agencies. He recalls for us the best job application letter he ever received – it was so different that twenty years later, he could still recite the first paragraph:

> My father was in charge of the men's lavatory in the Ritz Hotel. My mother was a chambermaid at the same hotel.
> I was educated at the London School of Economics.

He gave the writer of that letter a job as a copywriter, because he calculated that if someone could begin a letter like that he could make great advertisements.

Raymond Chandler, who created Philip Marlowe, the archetypal private eye, wasn't looking for a job but he was looking for a secretary. He found one with a classified ad that stood out from all the rest:

Non-U author desires the services of a private secretary
. . . salary liberal. Please send photograph, preferably in
the nude. Applicants should be university educated and
very refined. But not too damned refined! If interested,
please apply in writing, stating salary expected, height,
weight, age and colour of mink stole. This is an exceptional
opportunity. Don't miss!

Some management consultants believe one of the secrets of
Japan's extraordinary economic success is the constant striving
for innovation, which is just another way of saying striving to be
different. The Japanese were perhaps the first to wake up to the
breathtaking pace of post-war technological development, and
– as the 20th century races along – the importance of giving a
product in the shop-window some new advance, even a quite
minor one, to separate it from the competition.

One of the characteristics of competition in Japan is
the establishment of small distinctions between one's
own product and similar products made by other manufacturers.

Masanori Moritani, *Japanese Technology*

We should look at what we are offering, whether it's ourselves, a product, a service or an idea, and try to find something
different about it.

You may think this is difficult, if not impossible, but go
back to the drawing-board and have another look, because the
alternative is to *join the queue*. Then you might have a long wait.
Let's see how other people have done it – sometimes they may
have more on their side, but often it's just a simple idea.

A 'boardroom' sandwich service which started in a modest
way became a successful business in less than a year on the back
of a good idea: its innovators produced the 'Low-Cholesterol
Sandwich', their handouts stressing that every one of their
sandwiches was not only delicious but was low in cholesterol.
Health and heart conscious directors and executives were
hooked because who wants a heart-attack?

When Perrier launched their mineral water in the United States, they registered that all other mineral waters were advertised using beautiful lissom women, radiant and healthy. Instead of *joining the queue*, Perrier chose the least lissom, the least radiant and maybe the least healthy-looking of actors, Orson Welles. It was a marketing master-stroke, and sales of Perrier went up in three years from three million to a hundred million.

Glavcosmos, the Soviet Space Administration, had *being different* handed to them on a plate: they couldn't miss. But when they announced the first Anglo-Soviet space mission, lift-off 12 April 1991, requiring a British astronaut on board, they deserve credit for saying it as simply as possible in the headline of their whole-page advertisements in British newspapers:

ASTRONAUT WANTED
NO EXPERIENCE NECESSARY

After that example, perhaps you're looking glumly at the A4 sheet of paper in front of you, still virgin white. What can *you* say that can touch that for excitement and compelling drama? How do you *find* an idea?

Start off by trying out what writers and copywriters do, which is to write down something outrageously different, over the top in the unexpected. Of course you are not likely to use it in the final version, but it will get the adrenalin flowing. All creative people – writers, composers, actors, dancers – need to get excited over ideas: their hearts have to beat faster, their breathing must become more rapid.

When writers are working together, they often pace about in excitement, and wild let's-run-it-up-on-the-flagpole-and-see-who-salutes-it ideas come off the top of their heads. These are thrown out, new ideas come in and by some creative alchemy, the process narrows down to something that works. You can do this on your own by starting off with something you think is impossible, just to loosen up. More often than you might believe, 'impossible' ideas, when looked at again, turn out to be more possible than it seemed. An advertising agency in New York has opened a Risk Lab, where copywriters and art directors can work on way-out ideas. Not many of the ideas go any further, but they open up creative horizons.

When the pressure is on and you're looking either for an original idea, or the way to begin a letter, or how to make a report into something more than a static two-dimensional parade of information, open up your own Risk Lab. Take on a mood of creative excitement and see where it leads you. You have nothing to lose because you can always rein back afterwards; but if you start by reining-in, with shoulders hunched and blinkers on, you will end up with the expected and the ordinary.

The beginning of any communication – the first words you write, the first words you say – is your first chance to get to the head of the queue. Glavcosmos did it with their wonderfully simple headline, though of course they had something really exciting to say and you can be sure that was the one advertisement in the papers every reader looked at! A central heating firm supplying oil and servicing, did it by sending a letter with their account, which began 'We are advising customers not to pay our invoice'. In fact the firm was offering a budget-account facility which would enable customers to pay for oil and servicing by regular monthly payments.

Novelists know how important it is to grab their readers' attention right from page one. People will pick up a book in a bookshop, and often it is the first sentence on the first page that makes them decide to buy it. So writers work hard on the first sentence of the first chapter. George Orwell began his visionary novel *1984* with a sentence that promised us a book that was different:

It was a bright cold day in April and the clocks were striking thirteen. . .

Graham Greene's novels often start with a deadpan sentence or two that pull us up sharp. *A Gun For Sale* starts:

Murder didn't mean much to Raven. It was just a new job. . .

Anthony Burgess gave his novel, *Earthly Powers*, one of the most intriguing openings of all:

It was the afternoon of my eighty-first birthday, and I

was in bed with my catamite when Ali announced that
the archbishop had come to see me.

Could anyone not go on reading?

If it's good enough for famous and successful novelists to
work hard on their first sentence because a lot depends upon
it, it's worth our while to write and rewrite, think and rethink,
the first words we write or plan to say. Our first sentence is the
first chance to switch people on . . . or to switch them off. If
you can't think of something brilliant – and who *can* do this to
order every time? – here are some techniques that have been
proved to work.

Most people are immediately interested in something that
will *do* something for them, so see if you can *make an offer* in
your first sentence: 'Here is an idea that will save you a lot of
money . . . '; 'Here's a chance to get in on the ground floor of
something new . . .'; 'If you'd like to find out a way of getting
more done during the day without adding to the stress, just read
on . . .' Those opening sentences come from actual letters and
they all make you want to 'read all about it'.

Ask a *question*. By asking a question you engage the other
person. Research shows that a question in a headline increases
readership of an advertisement. You can use this simple device
in any communication – though of course it's important to
avoid questions that put people off, such as 'Can you lend me
a hundred dollars?' So find a question that is positive, that
they will be glad to think about: 'Would you like to pay less for
your petrol?' (the opening of a letter from a garage offering a
low-cost conversion to lead-free petrol); 'Would you prefer to
keep a customer instead of losing one?' (the first sentence of
a letter to the general manager of a department store from a
woman with a complaint); 'Would you help us to service your
order *today*?' (the beginning of a fax from a supplier to a new
customer, from whom more information was needed).

As usual in this book these examples are from real life. They
are simple enough, but they demonstrate how beginning with
a question involves someone else: they have to answer it, even
if only in their mind. It's a useful technique to use from time to
time – although don't fall in love with it and begin *every* letter
and fax with a question. Keep it in reserve for those times when
you're stuck for a good way to begin.

Ever since Periclean Athens, *drama* has been a way of getting and holding people's attention. A daring example of drama in communication comes from the Health Education Council, which took two consecutive whole-pages in national newspapers, a costly exercise but used to great effect. Filling the first page and looking straight out at us was a beautiful woman with lovely long flowing hair. The baseline:

**IF THIS WOMAN HAD THE VIRUS WHICH LEADS
TO AIDS, IN A FEW YEARS SHE COULD
LOOK LIKE THE PERSON OVER THE PAGE**

When you turned over, there was another whole-page advertisement with the same beautiful woman looking straight out at us. She looked *exactly the same*. The baseline:

WORRYING ISN'T IT?

That's an example of using a *question* to get attention. Some question! The brief copy explained that someone can be infected for several years with the Human Immunodeficiency Virus that leads to Aids, before showing any signs or symptoms. That advertisement could have come straight out of a Risk Lab – risks were taken, eyebrows were raised, tuts were tutted. But the drama of the idea rocketed it out of the crowd.

Now you've seen what drama can do, keep it as one of the options open to you to use when the chance presents itself. When this happens go into your own personal Risk Lab and see what you come up with.

Allied to drama is telling a story, even a very short one, even in a report – the most serious of subjects can be made more approachable by using a story to help us to relate to it. It's hard to imagine anything more serious and abstruse than the future of this planet we are all sharing. Stephen Hawking, who holds Newton's professorship at Cambridge, writes about this in his successful book *A Brief History of Time*. We open the book with trepidation, wondering whether we shall be able to stay with the highly complex arguments. To our relief, chapter one begins with a story: when Bertrand Russell (some say it was) gave a public lecture on astronomy, a little old lady at the back of the room got up and declared: 'You are very clever, young man, but what you have just told us is rubbish. The world is really a flat plate supported on the back of a giant tortoise'. We nod in gratitude towards Professor Hawking for easing us into a difficult subject.

There's no need to be hesitant about using a story as a way to bring statistics to life. Although we should be on guard against talking down to people, even experts will respond to a narrative, especially one with humour. In a previous chapter we used the story of Anne Ridgeway's day and were able to make facts about successful communication more colourful and vivid.

This practice can be effective even in business letters. There was one which began: 'The chief executive of a manufacturing company took the lift up to the sixth floor where he had his office and as he went through the door . . .' It was a letter about a clock-controlled coffee machine, so that a fresh cup of coffee can be waiting for you the moment you arrive!

It is right, of course, to be cautious about seeming frivolous over a serious matter, but if you are too solemn you run the risk of the people, who are listening to you or reading what you've written, switching off. A story can be as serious as the context calls for.

Getting someone's attention is one thing: holding it is something else. A good letter, a good report, a good telephone call keeps the other person with you *all the way*, so they take in the points you have to make. Unless you are a tone poet, or a theoretical physicist, or a computer freak writing for other computer freaks, the first step towards keeping anyone's attention about anything is to keep it simple. No-one wants to work any harder than they have to and it's our job, when we are communicating with other people, to make it as easy as possible. Among the glaring examples of how *not* to do it are many instruction books, which are not only difficult to find your way about in, but seem to be written, as one victim commented bitterly, 'by someone who has learned English from Lithuanian nuns!'

The most lethal of anti-communication weapons is the television remote-control switch – you only have to move your thumb a quarter of an inch and the channel is changed, or the set switched off altogether. Every one of us has an invisible remote-control switch that can be used against *any* communication. At any time someone can switch off their attention. From that moment on, you're wasting your time. If you're talking to them, you might be able to spot this switch-off from the faraway look in their eyes; but if they're reading something you've written, or listening to you on the telephone, you can't see them operate their inner remote-control switch.

You should be constantly aware of the *bore zone* and work on every sentence, every paragraph to keep out of it. For once you're in the bore zone, you're usually stuck there. John Harvey-Jones had a built-in plus when he was talking to people, for he was chairman of ICI; but even with that to back him up, he warns us '. . . once you lose your audience, you can never get them back'.

The best protection against the bore zone is to go over everything three times, to see if you can make it *shorter*. Cut out the odd word here and there if you like, but it is better still to cover up each paragraph, even each page, and see if you really lose much by leaving it out. When Kenneth McLeish wrote an obituary for the writer Bruce Chatwin, he said something that any writer would be glad to have on his tombstone:

> He revised each sentence to the glittering simplicity characteristic of one of our most immaculate contemporary stylists.

Lift out that phrase *glittering simplicity* and write it on a card – if that works for you – to keep in front of you when you are writing anything that is important. It's aiming high, but if you work at revising your own sentences, you can go some way along the road towards it.

> The thing that did my writing the most good was when I was badly off and paper was tremendously expensive. I thought I must think more about what I write. That did my style a hell of a lot of good.
>
> Mary Wesley

Sometimes a letter has to run into two, three or even four pages, yet it can still be effective, as with one notable example about a new investment system. There was a lot to explain because of the complexities of international stockmarkets; yet from beginning to end the letter held the attention of anyone who has ever invested in stocks. It succeeded because right from the start our own experience was involved, always a direct way of getting anyone's attention. It's sometimes called the 'I-know-this-has-happened-to-you' approach – listen to it at work:

> Let's face it, however well off you are, we all like that little bit extra from the stockmarket . . . However, since the crash it all seems to have gone wrong.

The writer goes on to wrap up the information step by step in a story, in the form of a telephone conversation with a stockbroker from which the idea for a system emerges. Once again it connects with our own experience:

> 'A system', I said, 'surely there's no such thing as a stockmarket system that really works.'

Nothing is rushed – our interest is held as the story carries us along with it.

Whoever drafted that convincing letter understood an important principle of communication: how fast to go. This is the guideline: it should always be the person we are writing or talking to who controls the pace at which information is given. It depends upon what the subject is, how much the other person knows about it, what their level of interest is likely to be and the surrounding situation. If we go too slowly, we end up talking down to them and slipping into the bore zone. If we go too fast, we lose them altogether.

Compare it to driving a car, with the passenger's foot on the accelerator so *they* can select the speed *they* want to travel at. If you're talking to someone, watch to see if you've got the right pace for *them*. If you're writing about something, keep in mind all the time the speed at which the other person will want to take it in. Timing is possibly the most important factor in almost everything we do, from investing on the stockmarket to making love. It plays a central part in communication.

When you want to bring out a special point in a letter, the obvious thing to do is to put it right at the end, so it's the last thought you leave with the reader. Wordprocessors can put something important into bold type, although at times that is too obvious. A useful option is to use the *afterthought technique*, adding a short note after your signature – it would be rather stuffy these days to call it a postscript. Positioning something at the bottom of the page gives it a special kind of emphasis by separating whatever it is from the rest of the letter.

Another way, even more effective, is to wait a day or two and send a follow-up letter, or a fax, simply saying there's something you want to add.

The First Direct banking service use this with great effect. They send details of the service to enquirers and if a month goes by without a response, they send a follow-up postcard headed: So you really don't want to open an account with First Direct? There follows a list of seven good things you'd be missing out on.

Research shows the *afterthought technique* works very effectively, that people do recall the special point that has been singled out. But once again, don't fall in love with it and don't try it too often on the same person!

There are people who write powerful and convincing letters, but seem to put on pince-nez and wing-collars the moment they sit down to draft a report. They spell *report* with a capital *R* and believe it has to be an imposing, solemn document that goes through all the options and ends with a long list of conclusions, qualified with judicious 'ifs' and 'buts'. Reports like that gather dust and end up ingloriously on the shelf.

Lee Iaocca, uncompromising boss of the Chrysler Corporation, gave this as one of the few invariable lessons he had distilled from forty-two years in the front line of business: 'Say it in English, and keep it short'. He backed it up with the story of a fifteen-page report that was hard work to get through – yet when he asked its writer to explain what he had written, he identified in *two minutes* what was going wrong and how it could be put right.

Reports usually include figures and statistics; so do letters sometimes. But always be careful how you present figures and how many you present. When Stephen Hawking wrote *A Brief History of Time*, he was warned that every equation he used in the book would halve the sales. It could not have been easy for the Lucasian Professor of Mathematics at Cambridge to take such advice to heart but Stephen Hawking did. He allowed himself only one equation in the whole book – no mean achievement in a book about advanced cosmology – and that was for the most famous of all Einstein's equations. Even then Professor Hawking was worried about scaring off half his potential readers.

Unless you are writing a report for accountants or economists or other highly numerate readers, every table or set of statistics you include will lose the attention of some of your readers. It is unrealistic to believe that *all* figures can be left out, as they are often essential to establish a case, but it is possible sometimes to make figures 'sit up and talk', to bring them to life for your readers. The slogan for British Airways is an example. In one year the airline chalked up a record 130,728 international aircraft departures. That statistic stayed flat on the page it was written on until someone thought of putting it this way:

THE WORLD'S FAVOURITE AIRLINE

When you have to include figures, look for ways of relating them directly to people. It's one thing to say that 25% of women going into a certain supermarket on Saturday mornings buy Brand X. It's something else to turn it into a story about people:

> If you stood outside this supermarket any Saturday morning, and counted a hundred women go in; and then looked into their shopping baskets as they came out, you would see a packet of *Brand X* in **25** of those baskets.

On their own, figures and statistics are like skeletons, and who falls in love with a skeleton? It is the flesh on the bones that attracts us.

Reports *can* be shorter, better, brighter, more interesting, easier to read – and easier to write when you know how to go about it. *The Review of Communication Skills* at the end of this chapter will remind you.

You can put a lot of hard work into writing something or talking to someone, yet not make sure you are communicating with the people who really count: *targeting* has already been described as one of the most important communication skills. In many cases, of course, you know without hesitation who it is you have to write to or speak to; at other times it is not so obvious. That's when you must work as hard as you can and take as much trouble as you can to find out the right person or people to aim at. Then you will have a head start, because you will be writing to or talking to someone who has the power to sign the cheque or say *Go ahead*.

Even advertisers with millions of pounds or dollars to spend are working much harder to reach the real potential buyers, instead of aiming broadside at the mass audience. They are using the capacity of computers to interpret a mass of complex data to help identify the individual characteristics of buyers rather than seeing them as an army of faceless consumers.

Most of us are not operating on that scale but we should always be prepared to give as much time as necessary to intelligent targeting. And be careful about *shifting goalposts*: the right person or people a year ago might not be the right ones today. Markets change, companies are taken over, responsibilities in organisations shift ever more rapidly to other people and other departments. In the 1990s every established idea is up for grabs, so when you are going through the targeting exercise, don't rely upon old information. Dodos are regular queue-joiners because they are out of date.

REVIEW OF COMMUNICATION SKILLS

1. Look at what you are offering, by letter, advertisement, fax or phone, and try to find something that makes it a little bit *different* from everyone else.

2. From time to time, go into your own personal *Risk Lab* where you can try out an idea, no matter how 'over the top' it may seem to begin with. Perhaps you won't use it, but you may adapt it. The Risk Lab opens up creative horizons for you.

3. Make your first sentence out of the ordinary. Here are three good techniques:
- Make an offer 'they can't refuse'.
- Ask a question.
- Try the 'I-know-this-has-happened-to-you' approach.

4. Look for a way of injecting *drama* into a communication. The old opening 'Something funny happened to me on the way to the Opera . . .' wasn't such a bad idea after all!

5. Remember that everyone who reads what you are writing, or listens to you, has a hidden *remote-control* switch and will switch off their attention if you make it too much like hard work. Make

what you write easy to read, what you say easy to listen to. Aim for *glittering simplicity*.

6. Read everything you write three times whenever possible to see if you can make it *shorter*. Deleting unnecessary words helps, but it's better to cover each paragraph and each page in turn, to see if you can manage without it.
   Be ruthless!

7. Reports that are shorter, livelier and more interesting are not only easier to read but are also easier to write. So everyone benefits.
   In your mind, spell *report* with a small 'r' – avoid going through *all* the options, to end with a long list of qualified conclusions.
   In a report, you cannot usually sidestep the responsibility of making a decision; if you try to do so, the report will not do much good either for you or for anyone else. Wherever possible, say *briefly* what is wrong and what you think is the best way to put it right.

8. Let the other person's situation, not your own impatience or expertise, decide how fast you should go in communicating with them.
   Timing plays a central part in good communication.

9. Keep the *afterthought technique* as an option for bringing out something important: put it in a sentence after your signature, or send a follow-up letter or fax, saying there's something you need to add.

10. Make figures and statistics 'sit up and talk' instead of lying flat on the page. Give them a personal meaning whenever possible, to help people relate to them.

11. Work hard at directing your communication as accurately as possible to where it can do most good. Look out for *shifting goalposts*: dodos are queue-joiners.

12. Write down straightaway one specific opportunity you expect to come up tomorrow when you can use a new technique, a new piece of knowledge, a new understanding you have read about in this chapter.

4 Wordpower in the 1990s

How to pick up the beat of the 1990s and make your communications, written and spoken, key into it
How to go into a meeting after a long journey – and function at your peak
How to use understatement
How to put snap, crackle and pop into your sentences
How to find words that relate to people

Powerful and effective communication, in any form, requires you to be in touch with the rhythm of the time you are living in. The Germans call it *zeitgeist*, a good word to remember as it's in most English dictionaries now. It embraces the whole trend of thinking, feeling and reacting to the characteristics of the years we are passing through. These form the backdrop against which our proposals, applications and ideas will be judged, and unless we take it into account we shall be outpaced by the competition.

If you are talking to astronauts in a spaceship, experiencing weightlessness, you have to remember where they are and what state they are in. All right, you may say, but that's not an everyday occurrence . . . *yet*; but it's not so far-fetched to be at a desk on the 27th floor of an office block in New York, talking to someone negotiating the traffic round Piccadilly Circus in London – or to be called by a customer on their mobile phone from a lunch table at Maxim's in Paris. This extraordinary mobility of communication is part of the 'spirit of the time', the literal meaning of *zeitgeist*.

This chapter sets out to put you in touch with how

communication, written and spoken, can key into the 1990s. If you pick up the beat, it will make it easier to accomplish the things you attempt. If you are perfectly in tune with it you could make a fortune, or be a latter-day Shakespeare, or at least be able to get your message across so that it really works for you, or enables you to help someone else.

As we move into the 1990s, there is a strung-up urgency about living. The thought of a new millenium, of the 21st century, is disturbing and arouses expectation. *2001* is no longer science fiction but the year we shall before long write on our cheques or punch out for our computerised cash transfers.

Top production-line cars – Porsche, Jaguar, Ferrari – already reach speeds well over 150mph and everything else is moving faster, with the human psycho-physical organism jet-lagging behind. New York has become a supersonic 'away-day' trip, a Concorde deal that gobbles up a mile every 2.5 seconds to take executives to the Big Apple for a four-hour meeting and get them back the same evening to sleep it off at home. The business centre at JFK airport completes the package by opening up conference rooms, boardrooms and everything you need either for a full-scale presentation or a one-to-one high-level negotiation.

It means that instead of flying twenty people across the Atlantic for a London meeting, we just need to feed them into New York for the day from Cleveland and Houston and arrange a single transatlantic ticket with no overnight stays.

Linda Romero, pa to
BP Chemicals' chief executive

These adventures, which may seem limited to top-flight executives whose time is at a premium, will become more commonplace as we move further into the last decade of this century. So we'd better learn how to handle them.

Techniques have been developed to help people who fly halfway across the world and come off the aircraft straight into a presentation to the board of a major company, or into a small conference room to convince someone of the bottom-line profitability of their proposals. Doctors and psychologists are retained to study how body and mind can accommodate the stress of travel, and leave us able to function at our peak the moment we arrive. The same techniques work just as effectively, even if your journey is limited to the short fast drive up the M1 to Birmingham or the milk-run flight from New York to Chicago.

We are taught that travelling is not dead time, when the body and mind are resting – nervous and physical energy are used up to adapt to the rapid transference from one place to another. It is not a calming reflection that when the leaders of nations arrive at the end of long tiring journeys, they are making decisions that can affect the security of all of us.

Of course there are things we can do to help, as we are advised, such as passing up in-flight champagne (even if it's 'on the house'!) in favour of mineral water, and there are relaxation exercises we can learn that minimise the effects of jet-lag. Switching into *awareness of your normal breathing*, the technique taught in chapter one of this book (see p16), as you leave your car or your plane on the way to a meeting, has been shown to be marvellously effective in inducing the change of pace and concentration you need after a journey, so you are ready for a presentation or negotiation.

It is always good, of course, to prepare for meetings in advance, and for interviews and discussions, but we are taught to prepare more thoroughly if our encounter is at the end of a long journey. Tests show it is better not to do this *on* the journey, but if possible the afternoon or evening before. It is explained at high-powered communication courses that preparation carried out the previous day becomes absorbed into the subconscious overnight, leaving you more in command of the situation the next day. If you leave preparation until the last minute, it is often counterproductive, inducing anxiety that will show in your face and your manner.

You will stay a significant jump ahead if you go so far as writing down, or dictating for transcription, the actual words you could use to begin a presentation or a meeting, and the answers to some of the questions that might come up. But do *not* attempt to learn this by heart, simply use it to prepare for the flow of a discussion. You can only go so far in preparing for any meeting, as you cannot predict what will arise or what questions will be asked; although it is surprising how often the prepared answers to one set of questions can be adapted off-the-cuff to deal with others. Every minute spent in preparation pays very good dividends: try not to skimp it, whatever the pressure of time.

One of the differences between people at the top and people who never get there is the willingness to work hard at preparation. It has been found many times that working in advance this way can actually make a journey less tiring because preparation lessens apprehension, which uses up nervous energy.

The vice-president of an international television news company who flies all over the world to negotiate deals, often has to be back with results the same day. His method of working is precise and unvaried: before a journey he lists the *results* he wants to return home with. He then works backwards to the steps he has to take and the arguments he has to present to lead up to those results. It makes sense: on any purposeful journey you should always know your destination in advance and plan the best route to get you there.

The same executive explained a useful ploy for setting up long distance meetings: the day before the meeting he sends what he calls a 'teaser-fax'. In case you haven't come across the expression, a *teaser* campaign is a series of advertisements or posters, even short TV commercials, that do not disclose the name of the product but intrigue and catch the attention of potential customers. When the campaign proper breaks, expectancy has been built up and the advertisements or whatever make much more impact. Have you ever kept a present for someone behind your back, so that when you bring it out, it's a real 'hey presto'? Simple stuff maybe, but if you've ever tried it, you'll know what an impact it makes.

A teaser-fax is not as obvious as that. The TV executive sends a fax to everyone he is planning to see, outlining what he is going to tell them – he includes enough to interest everyone, but keeps something back. The fax prepares the ground for him in advance, so that when he arrives and goes into the meeting he can come straight to the points he wants to make. It also arouses expectancy by suggesting he has new and exciting cards up his sleeve, the 'just-wait-until-you-hear-about this!' approach.

It takes practice to draft a good teaser-fax but if you get it right, it can greatly increase the results you get from a meeting or presentation when you arrive at your destination, whether it's at the end of a supersonic flight or a run-of-the-mill train journey. Here are four key questions to test a teaser-fax before you send it:

Will it interest them?
Will it leave them expectant?
Will it make them look forward to the meeting?
Does it leave you some rabbits to pull out of the hat?

If the answer is 'Yes!' to all four questions, send the fax and put your passport and airline ticket in your pocket: you stand a good chance of having a *bon voyage*!

So many communications in the 1990s have a tired look about them; we feel we've seen or heard it all before. Dictionaries long ago admitted as standard English the expression 'junk mail', to describe the unwanted, unread and often unreadable demands, entreaties and offers that thump on to our doormats. More and more executives are taking quick-reading courses in a desperate bid to keep up and skimming is replacing reading for many people, because there's no time for anything else.

Communication in the 1990s is beset by language inflation. A linguistic specialist has calculated that English now has a store of well over a million words. Just before the 1990s opened up, the new *Oxford English Dictionary* was published, its twenty volumes weighing about eight stone – over fifty kilos – and defining more than half a million words. Yet the Bible (Authorised Version) created the world and expounded the gospels using a vocabulary of not much more than 6,000 words. And Shakespeare used a 20,000-word vocabulary to leave us *Hamlet, King Lear, Romeo and Juliet* and the rest of the *complete works*.

How can you find your way through the verbal jungle of the 1990s, writing faxes, drafting letters, using words to win a contract or get a job? It is important to learn the difference between hype and positive convincing statements. Hype has succumbed to the universal law of diminishing returns: years ago David Ogilvy put us on guard against 'the filter that consumers erect to protect themselves against the daily deluge of advertising'.

Look for the possibilities of *understatement*, which can sometimes carry people with you more convincingly than banging the drum. The beginning of this letter of application for a job does that:

> It's likely you will receive applications from people who have higher qualifications and who may be more intelligent than I am. But it's less likely you will get an application from someone as determined as I am to give of their best to make this job a success for both of us.

The representative from an investment broker, explaining a new scheme, started by saying:

> There are good investments on the market that can undoubtedly make you more money than the scheme I am going to tell you about. They are tempting of course. Nor would I advise you against those investments.
>
> It depends upon how much *risk* you want to take. You will make less money with our scheme. I must tell you that in advance. But perhaps you will sleep more peacefully at night . . .

Low-key maybe but compelling stuff for anyone who has ever had their fingers burnt on the stockmarkets.

In the booming 1960s, the most successful estate agent in London achieved it all by nothing more than 'telling the truth, the whole truth – and even the unwholesome truth', as one of his clients described it. That's a rare talent when you are selling houses and apartments – though it must be added that the estate agent in question did it with panache and in great style:

> NEVER ANY PLANNING TROUBLE ABOUT *THIS* HOUSE. It's exactly like its neighbours, & nobody could ever accuse it of being original, interesting or even attractive . . . The gdn looks horrible, but so would you if you'd been neglected for 20 yrs. A fantastic bargain for the lower economic classes who don't take this sort of newspaper, but perhaps in the course of a fish supper . . .

> FILTHY OLD HOUSE – FASHIONABLE CHELSEA. Preserved as of Architectural Interest – God Knows Why. Providing you have enough patience and cash wld make 3 bedrms. 27ft L-drawing rm. a dining room, 1 or 2

bathrms, kit. The horrible patch of weed, refuse infected earth behind wld make a lovely Gdn – maybe.

FASHIONABLE ISLINGTON OLD CORNER BAK-ERY . . . Bake-hse/Workrm. behind. 2 cellars sordid enough to turn into club for tuned-in (or is it *on*?) dwarves. Big tatty living rm. on 1st flr. Rear Bedrm. in which squats THE BATH. 3 shabby rms. on top.

These advertisements were written by the late Roy Brooks, estate agent extraordinary, and enhanced Sunday mornings for readers of newspapers during the 1960s. Don't dismiss them as a joke, because *they worked*; Roy Brooks was described as '. . . beyond any doubt the best copywriter for property advertising in the history of the British press'. His advertisements were so successful that he could never get enough houses and apartments to sell.

It takes a lot of nerve to go as far as that but you can at least explore the possibility of telling the truth, without evasion or window-dressing. In the 1990s it would make a welcome clearing in the jungle of hype, and with judgement and intelligence it could lead to success. When you're up against it to find a new way of saying something, keep the possibility of telling 'the unwholesome truth' as an unexpected option. At least it would be an original approach.

Ever since the Renaissance, that gigantic transition in the mainstream of European thought and lifestyle between the 14th and 17th centuries, there has been an increasing confidence that human progress must come through science and technology. By the 1990s, nothing seems impossible; it can all be done by computers and high-tech. Customers will be able to feed their orders into computers, linked up by modems directly to suppliers' computers, which will automatically break down the finished goods required into components, requisition the raw materials, arranging payment through the computerised banking system, programme production in automated factories, print out invoices to customers and check on the payments received, all with hardly any human interference.

So who needs people? We all do, as much as ever, from an international conglomerate to the shop around the corner. And we need to be able to communicate with them, because people's inconsistencies and misunderstandings can – and do – go on throwing spanners into the most smooth-running of works.

Human instincts, feelings and perceptions repeatedly show that they can bring factors into our judgement beyond the range of any computer. It was his 'inner computer' that led the financier James Goldsmith to sell all his companies, shares, newspaper and casino interests in the summer of 1987, just a month or so before October when the world's stockmarkets crashed. It made him a Wall Street legend, put him on the cover of *Newsweek* and demonstrated yet again that people, and their individual reactions, are often the deciding factor in what will happen next.

In the 1990s and on into the 21st century our skills at communicating with other people, our ability to listen to them and to react sensitively to them will help us to anticipate the next moves in the game and will be a significant factor in deciding our success.

When you are trying to get people to work together, the big problem is that they don't know how to communicate what their problems are. Everybody gets terribly emotional and they are not able to express the problem clearly because it's so clouded and confused by their own feelings. So the problem still exists and it doesn't go away.

David Brown, manager of the biggest
photographic showroom in London

To communicate successfully you have to be alert to the pressures and the technological and psychological environment you are living in. So many of the words that communicate with us are depersonalised by computers and other automatons. Letters, articles and reports are keyed into wordprocessors and transmitted by telephone lines into fax machines. A journalist gets his story, say in Washington, taps it out on his lap-top mini-computer, picks up a telephone, uses a modem to transmit his copy immediately to the screen in front of his editor in London, who will edit and set it into column lines direct from the screen; he then sends it through for tomorrow's edition, which will be the first time he sees it in print on paper.

Wordprocessing, like food processing, can make for stand-ardised presentation. Susannah Clapp, assistant editor of the *London Review of Books*, feels that technology is leading to less contact between writers and their readers: 'Now it's as if all the copy springs from one giant brain'. But Roger Eglin, business editor of *The Sunday Times*, told me: 'It's a big step forward from the old days, when journalists filled up a waste-paper basket with false starts. With a lap-top computer, they just start writing'.

Yet perhaps it's too easy and something *is* lost on the way. In pre-wordprocessing days, Raymond Chandler, who has already given us good ideas, liked the mechanical resistance of typewriter keys: 'When you have to use your energy to put words down, you are more apt to make them *count*'. Some top executives who are working under constant pressure, will still, in some circumstances, pick up a pen and draft an important letter by hand. This approach isn't for everyone but if you are not confident about what has come out of a wordprocessor, it's an option you should keep open. When a situation looks ugly or challenging, see whether the direct line between your hand and your mind can help you find the words that will save the day. This may not be for you, but before you discard the sug-gestion because there's not enough time, remember that for some people, even people at the top, writing out something by hand is like turning the knob on a pair of binoculars: it brings a blurred image into sharp focus.

In any crisis, my greatest support is a clean sheet of paper and a pencil and the telephone off the hook.
Sir John Cuckney, chairman 3i Group and
Royal Insurance, *Advice from the Top*

Everyone in the 1990s is taking in more and more informa-tion from video screens, at work and at home. TV channels proliferate, entertainment and news are non-stop 24 hours a day. In France, hi-tech even provides sex, or at least sexual fantasy, via a VDU. *Minitel* is a mini-computer linked to a tele-phone line, and as well as more conventional information and services, it offers millions of frustrated lonely people eroticism through a keypad. They tap out their most intimate fantasies to never-to-be-seen dream lovers, sending and receiving messages which range from Kamasutra-like eroticism to crude do-it-yourself porn.

Other less exotic services are constantly adding to our dependence on video screens: the Shop TV service demonstrates thousands of different products to shoppers at home and home banking and leisure services are another VDU option. Video kiosks in some stores give pictures and detailed information about products, with customers keying-in orders, saying how they want to pay and whether they will collect the goods or have them delivered. Electronic publishing will allow people to read on-screen newspapers at home. More and more of our daily activities are being conducted through the cold gaze of a television monitor.

Research demonstrates that this increasing dependence on a video screen has an effect on our attention span and many people nowadays find it more difficult to give as much attention for as long a period either to words on paper or to person-to-person discussion. David Bernstein, a creative consultant on communication, believes 'the average attention span is down to five seconds and shrinking fast . . .'

Trailers for movies are frenetic in the feverish pace of cutting from one sensational image to another, to hook and hold the attention of the audience. Ad agencies are worried about the risk of boring viewers even in a *30-second* commercial! The BBC were a little more optimistic when they mounted a TV series called 'Three-Minute Culture', suggesting that three minutes is about the limit before boredom thresholds are triggered.

The situation is not as desperate as all this suggests and there is another side to the coin. Serious documentary programmes on television are watched by large audiences, more books are published than ever before and more people have seen Shakespearean drama in forty years of television than in four hundred years of the theatre. Yet we cannot ignore audience research, which shows that video entertainment encourages low-involvement attention: instant access is expected. Information is now exchanged about ten times faster than it was twenty years ago, the speed of cuts in the latest *Batman* or *James Bond* movie is much faster. This is the communication scene of the 1990s.

How can *you* fit into this scene and make it work? Wordpower now demands a more rapid rhythm in the use of language, and written and spoken English are moving much closer together. Yet there are people who still hesitate to use – at least in important letters and reports – contracted forms such as *I'm, I'll, you're, isn't, he's.* These forms are used freely now, even in official letters and documents. Respected novelists such as Graham Greene, Kingsley Amis and Edna O'Brien use them, not only in dialogue where they are natural, but also in descriptive passages. The way is wide open to use these and other shortened forms *in any context* to speed up the rhythm of your sentences.

Shortcuts are used to express figures and statistics: £5m, $10m. The computer term *kilobyte*, which defines units of computer storage, has led to the use of the abbreviation *k* as a quick way to say or write a thousand pounds or dollars: £20k, $100k (£20,000, $100,000). These shortcuts are familiar in newspapers and magazines and if you haven't got round to using them yourself, don't be the last to try them.

Readers and listeners expect sentences to be shorter. Comprehension tests show that people usually relate both written and spoken sentences to cuts in film and on television and film sequences are much shorter now. If someone has to read any one of your sentences twice in order to take it in, that sentence is probably not only badly written but too long as well.

It depends, of course, upon who you are writing for. If you happen to be writing a review for a serious literary journal, you don't have so much to worry about. But many people, including some chief executives and vice-presidents, will read or listen to us more willingly if our sentences have some 'snap, crackle and pop' about them.

A lot of people never think of using semi-colons (;) or colons (:). Both are useful to break up a long flow of words. Try them out occasionally to see how they feel: a semi-colon (;) has a touch of class about it; and a colon (:) can add an air of authority!

Few readers in the 1990s want paragraphs to be the long weighty affairs beloved by legal draftsmen. On the other hand there are sometimes serious proposals put forward where every sentence has a paragraph to itself. That's not necessary and could interrupt the flow of meaning. There's no rule about this and sometimes a very short or a long paragraph is justified. But if you've written four or more sentences without switching to a new paragraph (which is what I've just done), it's time to be thinking about it (which is what I'm now doing). . .

We have already listed brevity – using as few words as possible – as the best way to keep out of the bore zone and the pace of the 1990s makes this vital. Executives are working longer hours, some arriving at their desks by 8 o'clock in the morning and working into the evening. High-powered people resent wasting time reading more than is necessary. If they have to, the result is a negative reaction, which could be avoided.

There are chief executives, who can write their own ticket, who will sometimes return unread any recommendation or review that is not contained within a maximum of double-spaced lines on two sides of A4 paper. They contend that if the main points cannot be accommodated in that space, it has not been analysed properly. If that seems unreasonable to you, think back to the last time on a busy day when you were confronted with a three or four page letter or a thick report, and after struggling through it realised that the essentials could have been put down in half a dozen sentences.

The beginning and the end of a letter or report are usually the important parts and it is often the middle section that drags. A valuable lesson can be learned from the team which once assembled in a hotel room to work on a prime minister's speech before an important party conference. Ronald Millar, one of Margaret Thatcher's speech-writers, told us how they didn't know where to turn because they hadn't got a *middle*. An old hand at the game looked at what they had written: 'Stick the beginning and the end together,' he advised, 'Forget the middle!' That's often good advice. A lot of time and energy can be wasted writing or saying whole strings of double-indemnity sentences aimed at nothing more than keeping us off the hook of responsibility.

On some presentation courses you will be told about the 'three-or-five-reasons' approach. It's believed there may be an archetypal simplicity about dividing an argument or recommendation into *three* or *five* points. As children, *three* is the first 'complex' number we come into contact with. We learn our ABC, the three letters used to designate the alphabet, and continue to talk about the ABC of anything to mean a simple no-frills explanation. Then our first step in arithmetic is to learn to count on our fingers: one hand takes us up to *five*.

Such theories may sound rather tortuous, but experiments by cognitive psychologists show that three and five are numbers that we find reassuring, and remarkably convincing presentations have been built round this principle. See if your letter, proposal or report lends itself to giving three good reasons, or can be summarised in five points. In the hard competitive world where everybody is looking at the bottom line, it's no bad thing to have some primitive magic on your side.

When you are talking to somebody or to a group of people, the 'three-or-five-reasons' approach gives you a ready-made visual emphasis: you simply hold up your hand, count off the points, and your audience will take that image away with them! This could also apply to two or four, but according to some experts, those numbers don't connect in the same way.

Take it or leave it: if it does nothing else, it will stop you overloading your communication with too many points. Instead you will crystallise your message and focus on what really matters.

Even with the latest communications technology, most of us remain peculiarly dependent upon *words* most of the time. Yet the technological razzle-dazzle that carries our words to other people can make us careless about which words we choose. The risks are great: the wrong word can switch someone from being 'for' something to 'against' it, because words trigger off feelings. And more often than we may be prepared to admit, it is our feelings that produce the reactions that lead to decisions, no matter how much we tell ourselves we are 'thinking it out logically'.

As far as we know so far, technology affects but doesn't change the human condition. If someone finds a form of words that touches our heart and our imagination, we are more likely to go along with the suggestion. There is a doctor with many patients who are overweight, so he gives them a long talk and a diet sheet. If they don't seem to respond, he ends the consultation by saying: 'Every pound you lose gives you an extra year of life'. They're only words, but they give his advice a sharp turn of the screw!

Wordpower in the 1990s still depends on *how you say it*, just as it always has done. Words should never be taken for granted. A recent headline:

                        Wall St
                        plunges
                        45 points
almost caused a panic. An analytical poll showed that it wasn't
so much the drop in the Dow-Jones index, because other economic indicators were good – it was the use of the word *plunges*.
Outstanding communicators sweat blood to avoid using words
that will trigger things off in the wrong direction and to find
words that will have the right effect on people.

In a negotiation, the smallest and most insignificant word
can change the course of history.

> Sir Anthony Parsons,
> former British Ambassador to the UN

How do you test out an important word before using it?
There's a simple question that will guide you more successfully
than the biggest and most scholarly of dictionaries. You look
at the word you have chosen and ask: 'How does it *relate* to
the other person?'

The Marriage Guidance Council (the organisation formed
to help people over problems in their marriages) changed its
name to one word – *Relate*. This was a good decision, because
in communication *relating* is all. The Chairman of ICI, with all
his heavy commitments, found time to send *handwritten* letters
to members of his staff who had done well.

In the 1990s there are more people in the world to relate
to. It is daunting to reflect that in 1945, when World War
II ended, the number of human beings on earth was barely
half the figure estimated for the year this book is published.
Markets have become global, even for quite modest companies.
But no matter how diverse people are in their environment and
lifestyle, they want us to relate to them. The composer Arnold
Schoenberg, whose twelve-note scale makes his melodies so
obscure, wanted more than anything else 'that people should
know my tunes and whistle them'. Sadly for him, there's little
hope of that; Schoenberg's music is profound and complex but
you can't whistle his tunes.

You can whistle *Ol' Man River* but it is the *words* that

give it meaning. When a woman was introduced to the composer, Jerome Kern, at a party, she was excited: 'Oh, you're the man who wrote *Ol' Man River!*' she exclaimed. Mrs Oscar Hammerstein, wife of the lyric writer, was nearby and heard all this.

'Oh no!' she said, 'It was my husband who wrote *Ol' Man River*. All Mr Kern did was write the *da-da-di-da!*'

Even in the video-dominated 1990s, words are still important and can deliver the goods for us, when we learn to use them in the right way.

REVIEW OF COMMUNICATION SKILLS

1. At the end of a journey, on your way to a meeting, allow yourself to become aware of your inhalation and exhalation, without changing the rhythm. This technique, described in chapter one on p16, helps a great deal in reorientating us after a long journey.

2. Prepare extra carefully for a meeting that is to take place after a demanding journey, by working on it the afternoon or evening before you leave. Preparation the day before becomes absorbed into the subconscious, leaving us more in command of the situation when we arrive at our destination.

People at the top work harder on preparation. Good preparation lessens apprehension and makes a journey less tiring.

3. Write down the words you might use to begin a presentation, and the answers to expected questions. Don't learn them by heart but use them to put you in a purposeful state of mind.

4. Remember the international TV programme executive who lists the *results* he wants to return home with, and then works backwards to the arguments he will have to present to lead up to those results.

5. Set up a long-distance meeting with a *teaser-fax*, to prepare the ground for you in advance. But don't show your hand altogether: remember the 'Hey presto!' factor.

6. Look for possibilities of replacing *hype* by understatement – even 'the unwholesome truth', if it's presented in the right way, can put people on your side. At least keep it as a rare and original option!

7. In a crisis, try writing out something *by hand*, to see whether the direct link between your hand and your mind can help you find words that will save the day. People at the top, under great pressure, find time to do this.

8. The communication scene in the 1990s demands faster rhythms:

- Use shortened forms, such as *I'm, I'll, you're, isn't,* even in important letters and reports.
- Use shortcuts to express figures, such as £5m, $10m, £20k, $100k (for £20,000 and $100,000).
- Write shorter sentences.
- Try out semi-colons (;) and colons (:) to break up a long flow of words. See if they suit your style.
- Keep paragraphs short. If you've gone four or five sentences without starting a new paragraph, start thinking about it.

Not only breakfast cereals, but letters and reports can have *snap, crackle and pop!*

9. Whatever you're writing or saying, use as few words as you can – remember the 'two-sides-of-A4-paper' rule. Consider leaving out the middle and joining together the beginning and end of a letter or a report or a speech. The result can be dynamic!

10. Tests by cognitive psychologists show that *three* and *five* are numbers people find reassuring. So it's worth looking for ways of making *three* or *five* points about something you are putting up. Even if you don't believe a word about the primitive archetypal magic of numbers, the discipline will help you focus on points that really make an impact. And who knows . . . ?

11. Use words that *relate* to the people who will read them or listen to them.

Even in the video-dominated 1990s, words can still deliver the goods. But be prepared to sweat blood to find the right ones; all the best communicators do.

12. Write down straightaway one specific opportunity you expect to come up tomorrow when you can use a new technique, a new piece of knowledge, a new understanding you have read about in this chapter.

5 Human Skills

How to interact successfully with others
How to reduce stress and anxiety
How the latest medical and psychological research can help you to get things done
How to break bad news and deal with complaints
How to get through the barrier between you and someone else

What are 'human skills'? If you are not sure, you may be missing out on a decisive contribution to your success in whatever work you are doing. Let's assume that when you go into the office in the morning, or the factory, or the shop, you're competent and informed about the functional aspects of your work, you keep up-to-date with marketing appraisals, technical developments, and what the competition is up to. So far so good.

But what happens when someone comes in to see you? Or when there's a confrontational problem looming up with someone working for you, or with you, or with the person you work for? Or you have to see a customer? How much do you *know* about how to get the best out of other people? Or are you likely to fall back on being conciliatory or aggressive, not saying enough or saying too much? Will you find yourself halfway through the day with a tension headache, wishing that the morning had never happened or that you could go through it all over again, saying this, not saying that?

Learning human skills could make an extraordinary difference to the progress of your day. Through research and tests we know much more than ever before about how to work with others and this chapter lays out state-of-the-art knowledge on how to *relate* to people. Don't mix this up with 'managing people'. It's not telling them what to do; it's learning to understand them, learning how to get the best from them, which is also doing your best *for* them. They may be people working for you, or people you work for, or the people you live with: people are people whether they're on the shop floor, in the boardroom, or in your bed. In this chapter we explore ideas and tested practices that will help you acquire these skills, not to manipulate people but to work *with* them – which is another way of learning how to communicate.

In the 1990s, management consultants give human skills as much space in recommendations as cost-per-unit efficiency and marketing concepts. They form part of the studies for MBA degrees. And instead of assuming that we all know by some instinct how to work and live with each other, it's been found that learning the right skills greatly increases our effectiveness. Stress and anxiety which can make us ill are often caused by our interplay with others. When that goes better, there's a marked reduction in stress levels, both our own and in the people we interact with.

Job satisfaction is much more than just another fashionable catchphrase: doctors and psychologists engaged in occupational stress studies put it high up the list in preventive medicine, a significant contribution to avoiding coronaries and other stress-related illnesses. It is not over the top to suggest that learning human skills may save your own life and other people's.

Working . . . is about a search, too, for daily meaning as well as daily bread, for recognition as well as cash, for astonishment rather than torpor; in short, for a sort of life rather than a Monday-through-Friday sort of dying.

Studs Terkel, *Working*

Charles Handy, a visiting professor at the London Business School, tells us that the Japanese, whose global success at marketing technology has been so phenomenal, put human skills on the same level as technical skills. It is significant that some of the high-tech businesses in America are replacing the élitist title 'manager' by 'team leader' or 'project head', titles that suggest working together.

The *boss* syndrome produces results for a while, just as fear of dismissal will drive someone on, but these are limited, short-term approaches. We build on sounder foundations when we follow the advice of the chairman of ICI in Britain, to involve 'hearts and minds' if we want to make the right things happen at work and in our lives. But this chapter is not simply about pious goodwill towards all men and women. Human skills certainly recognise the importance of the individual, but they are also on the side of beating the competition, improving productivity, increasing profit margins and your own salary.

If you doubt that, remember 'human resources' has become an *in* phrase, even with financial directors – in the States there are vice-presidents of human resources. Shareholders have come to realise that most businesses are *people* businesses, where some of the most valuable assets go up and down in the lifts each day. Someone taking over a company is now likely to want an evaluation of its human resources, just as a company facing a takeover bid might want to show that the offer does not take into account the value of its assets that 'go up and down in its lifts'.

It's not only football teams that poach each other's players: head-hunters are constantly on the prowl, enticing away marketing directors, brand managers and others from one company to another. Finding people with the right skills has become a top priority in small and big businesses in every industrialised country. When you learn human skills your value goes up at whatever level you are.

Look through the 'Appointments' advertisements and you'll see these are written with the same copywriting drive as the ads for products competing in the marketplace. In the 1990s no company is too big or too prestigious not to have to sell itself to the people it wants to work for it:

> Emerge From The Darkness And
> Reveal Your True Potential

Perhaps your present position has failed to shed light on your talents.

Or maybe you joined a company which was once full of promise, but has only succeeded in clipping your wings . . .

(from an ICI ad)

WHAT HAVE THE
LAST TWO YEARS IN BUSINESS
DONE FOR YOU?

It's all too easy to settle for second best but don't you deserve more?

(from a Marks & Spencer ad)

We are all part of the human database and our ability to interact successfully with the other parts will affect every day of our lives at work and at home. When Ernest Hemingway called his novel about the Spanish Civil War, *For Whom the Bell Tolls*, he was borrowing the concept from the 17th century metaphysical poet, John Donne:

> . . . I am involved in mankind;
> and therefore never send to know
> for whom the bell tolls:
> it tolls for thee.

You would think Holiday Inns are light-years away from mystical poetry, yet William Walton, one of their founders, echoes the same idea in the American magazine *Healthy Companies*:

> Many executives touch and influence the lives of thousands of people . . . Their influence can build up a person or tear him down.

Being successful is getting things done and this needs a double focus: one focus in on the outside, perhaps on a market on the other side of the world maybe, or on keeping a local customer satisfied. But there must also be a focus on the inside, on the people working with us, the people we depend on, so that we get the backup we need.

Two business school academics, Nigel Piercy and Neil Morgan, talk about a company's 'internal marketplace': 'We have both internal and external customers'. They mean that both the people working *for* a company – the people behind the counter – as well as the people in front of it, have to be sold on a marketing plan, otherwise it won't work.

As always we must take this out of a business school lecture hall into our own lives. Most of the things we want to achieve need other people to help bring them about – think of it as succeeding in *your* internal marketplace. No business, from a mega-multinational to someone working from home, will survive for long without putting customer satisfaction first: that's the primary 'outer focus'. To achieve it, there must also be an 'inner focus' on everyone working with you – your suppliers, the fitter servicing your car, whoever answers the telephone . . .

How you relate to these people is likely in the long run to determine the outcome of what you set out to achieve . . . just as the success of this book depends upon how it relates to *you*. We are all in the same boat and the art of steering it, instead of rocking it, lies in our ability to learn human skills. How do we learn them?

The most advanced and practical knowledge on how to encourage people and get their support and cooperation is waiting for us, on tap once we have access to it. We find it in the more enlightened and progressive hospitals and in the medical departments of universities, where the relationship between doctors and patients has become the subject of painstaking research.

These skills are taught to both doctors and medical students and are available for us to use as well. They are not complicated and may even sound like commonsense, yet once they are brought to our attention, they can change every encounter we have.

Let's begin with something very simple, a real bedside case history, related by Dr David Mendel, a former consultant at St Thomas's Hospital in London. A group of students was doing the rounds in the hospital, presenting cases to Geoffrey Evans, a consultant of wide knowledge and experience. One student began his presentation of a patient: 'This case complains of . . .' Evans put a restraining hand on the student's arm.

'Just stop for a moment' he said gently, 'You've only spoken four words and you've managed to rob him of his identity and of his self-respect. He isn't *a case*; he's *Henry Murray*. And he doesn't *complain*; he is simply telling us what he is suffering from.'

The most important human skill is to see everybody as an individual, not as a unit that exists to carry out a function, but as someone whose reactions to what we say or how we look at them, will influence the way in which they respond to us. We'll take this concept away from the antiseptic smell of a hospital ward into a broadcasting studio.

The late Roy Plomley devised the long-running radio programme *Desert Island Discs*, in which each week a celebrity is invited to choose the eight records they would take with them if they were marooned on a desert island. His guest one week was the chairman of one of the biggest companies in the world.

'Our guest this week,' Roy Plomley began, 'is an industrialist, a company man.'

The chairman never forgot or forgave being written off into a category, instead of being introduced as a man who eats, drinks, makes love, has triumphs, failures and fears, the same as the rest of us. Years later, in his autobiography, he commented that Roy Plomley's opening remark 'switched me off a treat!'

If you think of someone only as 'your secretary' or 'your plumber' or 'your husband' or 'your son' or 'your boss' instead of a woman called Mary, a man called John, or a man who's just come back from holiday, it sets up the wrong attitude from the start, so when you talk to them, something is missing – that essential *relatedness* which not only makes our own life less lonely, but also gets the best from the other person.

Experts working with the World Federation for Medical Education believe that no matter how good a doctor may be as a technician and clinician, their skill at responding to patients, and getting response from them, may be the most important factor in deciding how quickly these patients will recover, or even if they will recover at all. There are consultants who think they're too busy for human preliminaries and insist on patients stripping and lying on the examination couch, even when they meet them for the first time. How's that for treating someone as a 'case for treatment' rather than as a human being who needs help?

We may not be curing people but we need the right response from them whether we're executives, lawyers, accountants, or whatever work we do. No matter how good we are at our job, we shall be more successful when we add the skills that enable us to motivate and encourage others. Don't think of this as useful peripheral training in the psychology of relationships; it's central to our ability to get a job done, to move on in our careers, or to make more money.

Good communication is not just about being nice and charming, because you can have bags of charm and still be a disaster . . . simple things such as courtesy and patience are important because they are about valuing people.
Penny Morris, fellow in communication studies,
Addenbrooke's Hospital, Cambridge

There are more things we can learn from research into medical practice: let's see what happens to prescriptions and then connect that to a day in our own working life. Dr David Pendleton, editor of *Doctor–Patient Communication*, estimates that of all medicines prescribed only a third will be taken correctly – another third will be taken in the wrong way and the last third rejected altogether.

Relate those estimates to your own week, in the office, on the shop floor or wherever you spend those long hours between leaving home after breakfast and letting yourself in through the front door in the evening. Suppose out of all the contacts you make during the day, a third are wasted, a third are ineffectual, and only a third really deliver the goods.

Maybe you feel you do better than that and of course that may be true. But what if an objective observer could be by your side throughout a working day, the way we joined Anne Ridgeway, marketing manager of Oxford Plastics (see chapter one, p17)?

At the end of your day, as you look through the observer's report, most of us would find that in almost every encounter we could have done better – at meetings when we were initiating or passing on instructions, discussions when we were seeking to convince, persuade or sell, even passing encounters when it was important to leave a positive impression or stimulate someone to do their best for us: in every case there could be an uncomfortably wide margin for stepping-up our effectiveness.

Apple Macintosh makes some of the most sophisticated

computers in the world. When you switch them on, the outline of a smiling face, drawn as it were by a child, appears on the VDU and a simple message greets you: 'Welcome to Apple'. People say they find themselves smiling back at that outline drawing! It's like getting up and going to meet someone coming into your office. Even high-tech finds it's good business to acknowledge that so much in daily living is a struggle for so many people. It starts with getting out of bed in the morning, continues through traffic jams or on crowded trains as we go off to face our work – and work itself usually imposes stresses and strains unnatural to the human organism, even if we have made brilliant adaptations to accommodate them.

This planet has – or had – a problem, which was this: most of the people living on it were unhappy for pretty much of the time . . . Many were increasingly of the opinion that they'd all made a big mistake in coming down from the trees in the first place. And some said that even the trees had been a bad move and that no-one should ever have left the oceans.

Douglas Adams, *The Hitch-hiker's Guide to the Galaxy*

Although we may try to put on a veneer of self-confidence, most of us need reassurance and encouragement, which is why high-tech has jumped on the *user-friendly* bandwagon. Remember for a moment how glad you were when you found a new piece of equipment made it just a little bit easier to relate to it, with far less struggle than you expected. Then remember that feeling the next time you have to deal with somebody at whatever level.

Remember this, too. All the chips in Silicon Valley cannot come within a mile of the reassurance and encouragement offered by gently touching someone's arm or looking them in the eye in a way that shows you understand their problem. Even if touching someone in this way does not come naturally to you, you may be surprised to find how much it does for you, as well as for the other person. Brian McAvoy, senior lecturer in general medical practice at Leicester University, puts a high therapeutic value on such simple gestures as 'the spontaneous hand on the shoulder'.

An experiment carried out in the psychology department of an American university tells us more. The correct number of coins were left in the slot of a cigarette vending machine. Someone comes along, finds the money, feeds it in and takes the packet of cigarettes. As they turn away, they are intercepted by a person who explains they left the money there by mistake and could they have it back, please.

Here's where the experiment starts. For a set number of cases the request – always couched in the same words and tone of voice – is made about three paces away from the other person. Then for the same number of instances, the same words and tone are used, but this time accompanied by a light touch on the other person's arm.

The difference was marked. Without the gesture, there was always hesitation and uneasiness. The light touch and closer approach overcame embarrassment and resentment, and the money was usually handed back with a smile or a disarming shrug. When you have something to say which is not going to be easy for another person to accept, try being a little closer to them, rather than on the other side of a desk: and look for ways of making a more human contact, either by the way you look at them or by a light touch. For some this comes easily; for others it needs practice – and of course we must always be on guard against false or conciliatory intimacy.

Doctors are often required to break bad news and they are now being taught how to do it in a positive way: this is always to put themselves in the other person's place. Lesley Fallowfield, lecturer in health psychology at the London Hospital Medical College, asks 'Who wants a doctor who is brilliant at analysing bloodcounts but can't talk to you?' She adds that as well as humanitarian reasons, there are sound medical grounds for learning good person-to-person communication because there is evidence that patients who are given bad news in the wrong way are likely to be clinically depressed for much longer. Remember that 'bad news' might simply be to tell someone that something has to be done again or that they have to work an hour later than usual.

Learning human skills is learning very simple things that make an extraordinary difference to working with others. Cary

L. Cooper, president of the British Academy of Management, gives this advice: 'Good managers learn how to praise'. His studies of British companies, carried out by an occupational stress unit, show that major problems of stress at work are caused by 'lack of caring and praise-giving skills'.

He tells us that Harold Tragash, director of human resources at Xerox in the States, suggests employees' productivity and health can be dramatically improved by praise and recognition. At Xerox, a 'You Deserve an *X* Today' scheme has been introduced for anyone who makes a special effort, for as you would expect, *X* at Xerox is the most important letter in the alphabet!

If we have learned by now that human skills start off with the simple recognition of another person's fears, problems and difficulties, then this is a giant step forward which could change every contact we make with someone else. Press-button technology submerges individuality, as we are all consigned to a database. This is the only way global marketing can function: international advertising agencies have their worldwide offices linked by computers and work out global advertising schemes to promote global brands. That's the drift in the 1990s. But we remain stubbornly individual and people still hunger to be recognised as themselves, as Bob or Joan or Philip or Helen. We are *I* and *me* to ourselves.

Build one-to-one relationships. How people feel about their manager determines what they are prepared to put into the job. Think how often we hear such expressions as 'I could work for that guy' . . . or the reverse.

Terry Lunn, personnel director,
Joseph Tetley & Son

There is an old adage that the best restaurant is one where the *maître d'hôtel* knows your name. 'Good evening, Sir' is all right, but if he remembers your name or finds it out from the list of reservations, and says 'Good evening, Mr So-and-so', we glow with warmth and expansiveness. We may not wear our initials on our blouse or our shirt – although many people do – but we like it when people know our name. Direct mail shots that begin 'Dear Customer', 'Dear Investor', 'Dear Houseowner', start off on the wrong foot and miss out on the first opportunity to make a person-to-person contact.

It's a part of human skills to know someone's name and to use it – not too often or people will think you're getting at them, but from time to time so *they* know you are talking to *them*.

Peter Stringfellow, a successful nightclub impresario, knows just how important people's names are – to them. He arrived on the London nightclub scene in the early 1980s and opened *Stringfellows* on the edge of Covent Garden. At the time, nobody had ever spent £1.5m, about $3m, on a new club in London.

The opening night was dazzling. Peter Stringfellow hired an elegant young man to stand by his shoulder and whisper the names of any notable who drifted in. 'So,' he said, 'I was able to shake everybody's hand and greet them by name. That's how we went.' And it went well, for there are now *Stringfellows* in New York and Miami.

But here is a warning, already hinted at earlier: false intimacy arouses uneasiness and suspicion. If you have ever disembarked at Casablanca, you will know that over-familiar greeting, as an unshaven stranger sidles up to you, puts his hand on your shoulder and says 'Hallo my friend!' No welcome could be more chilling. Less sinister, but with the same phony ring, are those television commercials that seem too cosy, too confidential, too personal.

Your interest in the other person must be genuine, or the very way you use their name will be a giveaway. If this interest doesn't come naturally to you, here are ways to bring it to the surface – these are taught at courses on human skills. You can think of them as tricks, if you like, but the purpose is to get through the barrier between you and another person.

As you talk to someone, think what it is like for them returning home at the end of the day – or think of them struggling to get up in the morning. It will probably be imaginary of course, but no matter. And don't dismiss these ideas as far-fetched, because they have a way of putting something into your tone of voice and into the way you look at someone, that encourages them. Try this for yourself, to begin with in situations that are not so important, such as talking to someone serving you in a shop. It will help you to see someone as an individual; in turn, that person senses you are interested in them and responds to that.

When we have to say something unpleasant, evasiveness never gets us off the hook for long and usually arouses distrust. Bad news is bad news and we should not cover it up, although we can look for a positive aspect. On one course, this is described as 'the-bottle-is-half-full-rather-than-half-empty!' approach.

Courses in *assertiveness* are starting up everywhere. At first these were mainly for women, who felt they had to learn to assert themselves in work situations mostly dominated by men. But more and more men are enrolling for this training, lawyers, accountants, advertising executives, who want to learn how to put over themselves or a point of view more effectively.

Assertiveness is a human skill because it must always relate to other people. Aggression and table-thumping are not the same thing, because although they may at times bring about compliance, they seldom get people on your side. What is often taught about assertiveness is that it should be seen as an arrow with two heads, one pointing inwards towards yourself, the other outwards towards other people.

The inward-pointing arrow shows that the first step comes from us: we must stop to analyse clearly *what* we want to assert. This is often lost sight of and assertiveness becomes an end in itself, instead of being directed towards the end we want to achieve. Assertiveness is *not* projecting our own ego – it is getting the right response from someone else and this is the theme of the courses and seminars designed to teach it. The outward-pointing arrow shows we have to take into account the needs of other people and make out our case so those needs are met. If you are selling something to people, you will only succeed when *they* feel they want it. If you need people to carry out the next step in your plan, you have to get their willing response – unless you've got a gun and that's aggression, not assertiveness.

Assertiveness is about being able to deal with a difficult situation in a way that allows you to express your views, but leaves you and hopefully the other person feeling comfortable.

Kay Lily, teacher of assertiveness,
City of London University

The skills described in this chapter may seem simple but they are distilled from lectures, seminars and discussions with experienced psychologists and management consultants. Top executives, presidents of companies and even Heads of State spend time and money learning them, because they can significantly influence success.

For our last lesson we go back into a broadcasting studio. Rabbi Lionel Blue is often allotted the Monday morning slot by the BBC for the five-minute 'Thought for the Day', at prime listening time just before the 8 o'clock news. Those five minutes have made him one of the most popular of broadcasters, and people of all faiths – and of no faith at all – switch on the radio to hear him, because Rabbi Blue has learnt to offer people the simple things they need:

> My aim on a Monday morning is to give people the courage to get out of bed because that's what they need then. When I've learnt how to do that, I might go on to something slightly bigger.

This ties in with the advice given earlier, to think of someone getting out of bed in the morning as we talk to them. The problem of getting out of bed – especially on a Monday morning – which Rabbi Blue identifies, is something we share with everyone we work and live with.

REVIEW OF COMMUNICATION SKILLS

1. Work at seeing people as individuals, not as units that exist to carry out a function you need. Remember we are *I* and *me* to ourselves and that a personal reaction will affect the way someone works with you or for you.

2. We have *internal* as well as external customers, the people *behind* the counter, as well as the people in front of it. Take fully into account the people working with you, for you, or above you, whose support you need for 100% backup.

3. Remember the smiling face on an Apple Macintosh VDU and the message: 'Welcome to Apple'. There's some evidence to show that it has a good effect on people. See if you can adapt the idea.

4. High-tech is jumping on the *user-friendly* bandwagon. But remember, all the chips in Silicon Valley cannot come within a mile of the reassurance and encouragement offered by gently touching someone's arm and letting them see you understand their problem.

5. When you have something unpleasant to communicate, avoid evasiveness and see if there's a positive side: *the-bottle-is-half-full-rather-than-half-empty*! approach.

6. Learning human skills is learning very simple things, the simple recognition of the other person's fears, problems and difficulties. That's a giant step forward which could change every contact you have with another person.

7. Serious problems and stresses are caused by not telling people they have done things well. Remember Xerox's 'You Deserve an *X* Today'.

8. It's a human skill to know a person's name and to use it from time to time when you're talking to them, so *they* know you are talking to *them*. But be on guard against overdoing it.

9. To break through the barrier between you and someone else, try this experiment devised by a psychologist: as you are talking to a person, think what it is like for them to be returning home tired at the end of the day – or imagine them struggling to get up in the morning. It has been discovered that this simple approach can put something into your tone of voice or the look in your eye that will encourage that person to respond to you.

10. Assertiveness is an arrow with two heads. One head points inwards to remind you to analyse clearly *what* you want to assert: the other head points outwards to remind you to take into account the needs of other people, and to make out your case so those needs are met.

11. Write down straightaway one specific opportunity you expect to come up tomorrow when you can use a new technique, a new piece of knowledge, a new understanding you have read about in this chapter.

6 Talking to People

*How TV interviewers' techniques can help you key into someone's reactions,
    so you know what to say next
How to prepare for an important meeting so it works like a dress rehearsal
How to steer round objections and get a positive response
How to deal with stress
How not to say too much!*

**Some years ago I was in a railway carriage, travelling west
out of Chicago.** The only other passenger was an attractive
woman, a blonde I irrelevantly recollect. We were strangers,
a fact I regretted. The train stopped between stations and it
seemed as if we were in for a long wait. After a few minutes
of this, I glanced across at my fellow traveller and introduced
myself, saying 'It looks as if we're going to be stuck here together
for some while, so if it's all right with you, perhaps we could
talk to each other.'

'It's all right with me' she answered.

'Is there anything you would like to talk about?' I asked.

She thought for a moment or two, smiled and said: 'Talk to
me about *me*!'

So I did.

What does this true, modestly romantic story have to do with
the hard thrust of business and negotiations? *Everything*: and the
truth it contains has been proved time and time again. Here's
one proof, the greatest success story in the history of advertising.

When the Saatchi brothers opened their small creative 'hot-
shop' in London in 1970, they broke away from the traditional

ad agency presentation to prospective clients. The standard practice was this: as soon as the client came through the front door, they were confronted by an elaborate presentation which the advertising agency mounted to explain everything about itself. They showed creative work, illustrated success stories for other clients, charted the increase in the agency's billings, detailed the experience of their top people and so on . . . and on. If the client was bored, never mind: the agency put as much as it could into its shop window.

Saatchi and Saatchi turned their back on all that. When a client came in, they started off right away talking about the *client's* problems, the *client's* opportunities, charting the possible upward curve of the *client's* sales graph. They recognised an essential fact about human nature, that the attractive blonde expressed so irresistibly in that train out of Chicago: we are to ourselves the ever-interesting topic, the subject that never bores.

In less than seventeen years Saatchi and Saatchi's small creative 'hot-shop' became the biggest advertising business the world has ever known. Although the Saatchi international conglomerate ran into serious financial difficulties in later years, nothing can detract from that extraordinary achievement and the 'talk-to-me-about-me!' principle had a lot to do with it. That same principle will not only change the quality of your communication with other people, it will make you a better grocer, a better vicar, a better salesman, a better department manager, a better doctor.

What patients want of a doctor is concern with their own affairs. You have to listen to them and actually be interested in what they are saying, and actually want to know what they think and what is troubling them . . . This sort of mutuality is impossible if you have previously been led to believe that you are the star and that their job is to admire.

David Mendel, *Proper Doctoring*

Of course we also have to talk about ourselves and what we want and what we need. But we should always make the attempt to relate this to the other person. A production manager was on a personal visit to a supplier because he desperately needed delivery of materials well ahead of the usual time. That's what *he* wanted and he said so. But he added:

If you can do this for us, I can tell you this: you will have got a customer for life! What's more, we'll settle your account the same week.

Those were things *the supplier* wanted.

Talking to somebody effectively always depends on the effort we make to relate to them. The word *relate* has already been used more than once in this book and it will come up again, because communication *is* relating. There is no better guide to what to say next and how to say it than switching on to the *other person's* reactions. Dr David Mendel, the consultant whose knowledge and experience have contributed so much to this book, says his work is 'a never-ending study of patients' reactions, requirements, fears and feelings'.

The next time you watch a television interview, notice how important *reaction shots* are, those cutaways that show us how a person looks when something is said to them or a certain question asked. Reaction shots can be so revealing that in the States, when top-level political confrontations are on television, there's sometimes an agreement with the director about 'no cutaways'. Otherwise the audience might see senators wiping the sweat from their brows, or droplets dabbed away from a presidential upper lip. In Britain, to begin with, directors were not allowed to use reaction shots when the proceedings of the House of Commons were televised.

When we're talking to someone, especially to a group of people, we're giving a kind of performance: our audience is the other person. Peter Brook, one of the most dynamic of theatre directors, never ceases to teach his actors to respect audiences and to learn from them '. . . whether throbbing with excitement – I think of three hundred black teenagers in Brooklyn; or menacing, stoned on glue in the Bronx; or grave, immobile and attentive – in a Saharan oasis'.

We are not likely to be exposed to such extreme demands, but even in a simple conversation either at work or at home, the same lesson is to be learned: think about and respect *the other person*. That can change everything and can open the door to an agreement, a sale or a contract.

Actors have to keep to a script written in advance, although they can still modify tone, gesture and rhythm in response to reactions. We can do much more: we can actually change the script if we see it is not getting a good reaction. You can spend as long as you like preparing and imagining what you are going to say to people, but when you are face to face with them, you may not be able to use the script you have so carefully worked out. Every encounter brings with it the need to improvise, and reaction shots are not only for television: *we* can learn to look for them every time we're talking to someone. And when this becomes so much a habit that we drop into it whenever necessary, it is a remarkable tool in negotiations or discussions.

The mere words you use will be empty and valueless. They gain life and meaning only when you take into account their numinosity, i.e. their relationship to the living individual.

C G Jung, *Man and His Symbols*

Think back, and you will find that nearly every major step you have taken in life has come about through *talking to people*. Now think forward, to the things you want to accomplish, and you will find that the point of departure is so often how you talk to someone.

Wouldn't it be marvellous if we could rehearse in advance a difficult encounter we have to face the next day, and then look at a videotape playback? We would see close-ups of the other person's reactions, shots of our own expressions and we could listen to the tone in our voice. We could work on all this so that when we go into pitch for new business, argue for an increase in salary or whatever other thing is important to us, we know how to handle it in the best way.

But instead, our interview or meeting is dress rehearsal and the real thing rolled into one, and usually it's a one-night stand – we don't get a second chance. How can we stack more of the cards on our side? If we know how, it is possible to go a long way towards getting all the benefits of a rehearsal. What follows is the method taught at some of the top business schools in the world.

Preparation is everything, just as an actor works in advance at understanding the role he's going to play. You prepare for the meeting – though not to the extent of fixing every detail, because you cannot be sure how it's going to develop, any more than an actor knows the responses he will get. But you visualise possible reaction shots, and work out in advance how to deal with them.

As the discussion or meeting proceeds you key into reactions. Think of yourself as being in a TV control room, cutting to close-ups of the other people. That's a good technique, as it jolts us into looking for reactions – and reacting to them ourselves. Very few people are completely poker-faced, and as you train yourself to look into their eyes, at the nature of their smile or the tilt of their head, you will tune in to advance signals. Think of these as cutaway shots that enable you to adapt your script to steer round objections. Television interviewers have trained themselves to work in this way, so they can anticipate the question to ask next.

This requires thinking quickly. But it has been established that most of us can speed up our thinking far beyond our usual rate, just as we can step up our reading speed. Switching into a higher gear of attention is often enough to start the process. These are skills to work on. The world's most successful negotiators have acquired them: you can too.

Begin with ordinary everyday situations – buying a newspaper, having coffee with a friend, talking to a neighbour – so you learn the method in a relaxed way. Then it's ready for you to use when something really important is at stake. By practising these simple skills we can all become immeasurably more effective at talking to people, and once the skills become part of us, they serve us for the rest of our lives.

The same method works if you're trying to help somebody or teach them something. Be on the alert to catch their reactions, and you will learn to see the right moment to encourage or inspire them, or to explain something in another way. And as you get used to this, every conversation you have will become more alive, every meeting more effective, every contact with another person more vibrant.

Einstein's general theory of relativity put an end to our concept of time as absolute and fixed; from then on, time became dynamic and relative. These are cosmological considerations, which may only come into our head when we're looking up at the sky on a clear starry night. Down to earth, most people still see communication as absolute: they write something or say something and see it as fixed and meaningful in its own right. They are wrong: communication is *also* subject to the law of relativity. It is relative to the person at the receiving end: the act of communicating is only complete when someone else is affected by it.

This book needs two people to bring it to life. I'm one of them because I'm writing it and the book would not exist without me. You're the other, because you are reading it and without you the book would lose its purpose and energy. Communication always requires at least two people. Talking to yourself may be meditation, or sometimes madness, but it is never communication. Yet often people are so focussed on what *they* are saying that it's almost like talking to themselves.

Nearly every failure to get a message across or to convince someone is because the other person has not been taken properly into account. There is one course on communication which invites you to conjure up a mental image of a person blindfolded, trying to shoot at a target. That, you are told, is what it is like when you're talking to someone and not focussed on them.

What happens when two people meet? You could simply say that Philip meets Stephen or Mary meets John, but that is only the 'tip of the iceberg'. A meeting between two people is a coming together of a whole spectrum of psychological forces. It is a meeting of different attitudes, countless different experiences, a gathering of different fears. But – and this is what we have to single out – it is also a meeting of possibilities.

Kevin Goldfarb, partner in a leading firm of accountants, explains that much of their work is on the telephone and by letter and fax. So they make a point of arranging informal meetings at their offices, over a drink in the evening, with people they might not otherwise meet, such as solicitors, consultants, even tax inspectors, because, as Kevin has found, 'Once you've met somebody, you can break down the barriers'.

What are the barriers between us and someone else? Psychologists explain them as *projections*: when we meet someone we tend to project on to them an image of what we think they are like. It may be the image formed by the way they look, the way they are dressed, their accent, or what we have come to expect of people who do their job. It is like meeting a blank screen on which *we* project our own prejudices and feelings. If we allow ourselves to be stuck with that projected image, we end up talking to a figment of our own imagination instead of to the real person sitting opposite. We talk to our own conception and, above all, to our own fears.

This may seem a strange idea to you, but it is a psychological truth. It causes breakdowns in negotiations at all levels, as well as rows between wives and husbands and misery and misunderstanding between parents and children.

Here is a powerful exercise to enable you to see the projection principle at work in your own life. It was devised by a psychotherapist of wide experience and with exceptional understanding of human nature. Before you meet someone for the first time, or even someone you have known for years, write down or go over in your mind what you *think* you know about them. Then review your list and ask how much more there is that you don't know about. As you clear away illusions and prejudices, the way is more open for you to talk to the real person.

Let's put this exercise into practice and see how it helps us to talk to people more directly and more effectively. The head of your department has asked you to come in to see them at 11am the next day. You're not sure what it's about but feel it must be some criticism of the way you are doing your work. What they think or say can affect your wellbeing and your future.

You are projecting on to *them* an image of authority and power, an image formed by *your* doubts, *your* fears. At 11 o'clock next morning you go in to talk to that projected image, and inevitably this affects what you say and how you say it.

Now try moving all that out of the way so you see the real person, say John Birch, aged about 50, slightly overweight, under pressure maybe to keep a board of directors happy or to keep customers satisfied. As you work at this exercise, you find yourself entering John Birch's office in a different way, talking to him on more equal terms, and perhaps for the first time meeting the man behind the mask, the mask *you* put there.

In *Human Skills*, the previous chapter, we examined how stress and anxiety are often caused by our interplay with other people. Many doctors believe stress plays a much more significant role in heart disease than high blood levels of cholesterol. John Hunter, a famous 18th-century surgeon, may not have known about cholesterol levels causing spasms of the arteries to the heart, but he knew about the dangers of fear and anger. He once said 'My life is in the hands of any rascal who cares to make me angry!' He was right, because soon afterwards he died after a row with a colleague at St George's Hospital in London.

If you are reading this book in the evening after a day's work, stop for a few minutes and review your day in the office, factory, shop or wherever, and examine in particular how much *stress* has been caused through encounters and discussions with people. It could be a few moments well spent, because an understanding of stress can add years to our lives. Freedom from stress is one of the secrets of longevity – allergies, stomach upsets, poor sleep and more seriously, heart and kidney diseases, can all be related to stress.

Hans Selye, an Austro-Hungarian doctor, developed a theory of stress as far back as the mid-1930s. Selye believed that stress in itself does not make us ill; it all depends upon our ability to handle it. The principle he taught was to fight as hard as you can to achieve what you want, but learn to recognise the moment to stop.

In any important discussion, we are usually seeking to convince or persuade someone to 'see it our way'. We may succeed, particularly when we present points so they have value for the other person. But sometimes a stage is reached at which no further progress can be made and when we go beyond that point, we invite tension and stress.

We can develop the skill to perceive when to stop. This is not the same as taking 'no' for an answer too soon: it is knowing when 'no' is the only response we are going to get, at least that time round. If we gently stop the discussion at that point, or change the subject, we may preserve goodwill and keep the door open to bring up the matter again. Banging your head against a brick wall is bad for your health.

There is a technique for ending an encounter that is leading nowhere, which is taught at management seminars. You wait for a pause and then ask: 'Would you mind if I send you a short note just setting out the main points?' Keep this approach in reserve for when the going is too rough to get anywhere.

Asking a question, rather than making a direct statement, can sometimes help to sidestep antagonism. Pierre Boulez, the French composer and conductor, as much at home in London as he is in Paris, said about William Glock, the BBC's controller of music at the time, 'He would never tell you "You're wrong!" Instead he would ask the question: "Don't you think we could try . . . ?"'

If you manoeuvre someone into a corner, the only way out for them is to *fight*. By asking a question, you allow them room to manoeuvre and the door remains open to an agreement, or at least to a compromise. Even if you are the boss or the head of a department, winning an argument doesn't always mean winning the day. Macho-management belongs to the past. In the 1990s the long-term success of a business, whether it's employing a 50,000 workforce or only half-a-dozen part-time helpers, depends on understanding how to involve the feelings rather than the fears of people working with you. Even the toughest approach can command only a part of their effort; the rest will be given because they *want* to give it. The frontiers of human limitations can be pushed back, when we learn the skills of talking to people.

One person talking to another involves a lot of human machinery. The psycho-factors that affect the way we influence and convince another person are being studied in a new theory with an awesome name: *neuro-linguistic programming*. In some ways this is a highly developed form of applied psychology, based on intensive research into microscopic details of our patterns of behaviour when we are talking or listening.

Neuro-linguistic programming originated in the United States, where there is a Society of NLP; but a European Institute of NLP is now also established. NLP sets out to break down communication into every detail of the way we reveal what we are thinking and feeling by how we behave, how we sit, the words we use, our eye movements, breathing, gestures and almost everything else the human body can manifest. It is claimed that when we learn to understand these behavioural patterns, we get through to a much higher level of communication.

The impressive list of companies interested in NLP in management training suggests there is something in it for all of us. British Telecom is running NLP workshops and Rank Xerox, ICI, Holiday Inn, IBM and the British Department of Customs and Excise are all experimenting with it.

> NLP gives you a piece-by-piece analysis of interaction
> ... NLP focusses on internal growth and development.
> It provides a structure for people to develop new thinking
> processes.
>
> Dudley Masters, director UK Training

Neuro-linguistic programming is taught at expensive courses for management consultants and this is the way to study it in depth. But long before NLP was formulated, the way we unconsciously reveal our inner feelings and reactions through body language was studied by psychologists and anthropologists. In this chapter, we isolate important aspects you should know about.

We cannot conceal physical manifestations of emotions and thoughts: the mind relates to the body, the body to the mind. Our desires, hopes, fears, loves, have corresponding physical phenomena: in most men, a sexual thought involuntarily produces an erection; if someone puts their hands on their hips they are likely to argue with you; if they fold their arms they are probably on guard or on the defensive. This may seem low-tech stuff, but when we learn to read signals in others, and in ourselves, it adds important new skills to our ability to talk to people effectively and successfully.

It's a significant step, and one that can change the way you communicate with someone, when you work at getting to know how body movements, facial expressions and tone of voice convey mood. It gives you greater freedom in the way you communicate and extends your understanding of others.

> By the time we are adults we are all highly sensitive to the
> tiniest changes in expression, gesture, posture and bodily
> adornment ... If we took the trouble to make a more
> analytical study of body appearances we could become
> even more sensitised to them ...
>
> Desmond Morris, *Bodywatching*

While you're on a train, practise 'reading' people's faces as they are talking to one another and see what you can pick up about their reactions. With a little practice, our ability to 'read' faces increases surprisingly quickly.

More than anything else, the *eyes* can tell us what is passing through another person's mind and can reveal thoughts and emotions that the other person may not even be aware of themselves. For the eyes are a window on the unconscious mind, and it has been said that our pupils, those black spots at the centre of our eyes, cannot lie.

Nothing relates us more closely to another person than looking them directly in the eyes. If you make a habit of studying eyes and interpreting them, it will help you in every relationship you have, whether it's with a customer or with someone you love.

This is not the same as looking someone in the eye mechanically, simply because we know that's the right thing to do. It's looking and *registering* what you see. Many people are embarrassed or afraid to do this; the contact is too intimate and they back away from it. If you feel that way, begin cautiously: look and interpret for only a second or two at a time and then switch off. You will build up confidence that way to work for longer periods.

Watch the way in which someone's pupils dilate and contract; this is a remarkable guide to another person's response. As we interest people more, especially if they like what we're saying, their pupils expand – but if we switch them off by something they don't like, their pupils contract. When we say someone 'narrows their eyes', we mean they are showing resentment or suspicion. This is language clearly expressing – as it so often does – a psychophysical truth.

All this has to be worked at gently and sensitively as a method of understanding someone and relating to them as another human being. Staring at someone too intently for too long can become threatening, so look away from time to time – or if they become uneasy. This is assuming, of course, that you are not deliberately out to confront, which is another matter.

When you are saying something important – selling a product or an idea or a service – that is the moment to look the other person directly in the eyes, for if you look away then, it will encourage doubts.

The *mouth* comes next as a guide to reactions: the human

mouth is not only functional, it is extraordinarily expressive. When people purse their lips, we know they're not responding to what we are saying and that we'd better look for another angle. But when they part their lips in a friendly smile, we're on the winning side. The mouth has been called 'the battle-ground of the face'.

A nervous smile will tell you if someone is on the run. If this is not what you intend, then it is the moment to reassure and encourage them. A mechanical smile that doesn't extend to the eyes and the rest of the face, is a warning you are not getting anywhere, that the time has come to find a new approach. Smiling works both ways, and *you* can use a smile to encourage and reassure someone, to help them accept something you have to say. Psychoanalysts maintain that the way a mother smiles at her baby gives her child confidence in later life. A smile shows you are pleased to see someone and suggests you are confident and approachable.

Being able to smile at the right moment is very useful: if it doesn't come easily, look at the technique used by television presenters – it's described in chapter two and outlined in point eight of the *Review of Communication Skills* on page 38.

Kant called the human hand 'the physical part of the brain'. The way we use our *hands*, consciously and unconsciously, expresses a wide range of ideas and emotions: we salute with them to express respect of rank, we wring them to express distress, clench them to express defiance, extend the palms upwards to convey welcome. Generally if people fidget, it's a sign of anxiety; if their hands are relaxed and still, it's an encouraging sign of trust and interest in what you are saying. These are not hard and fast rules, of course, but in the complex process of one person talking to another, every straw in the wind can guide us.

It's just as important to be aware of the way we use our own hands, often unconsciously. There is evidence that if we put a hand to our mouth – or in fact anywhere on our face – it conveys doubt or uncertainty. Our hands are marvellously expressive and reveal negative as well as positive feelings. One discipline taught at courses on public speaking is to spend a few minutes making a point of observing what we are doing with our hands. If we do this from time to time during our working day we become more aware of them and how to use them to express positive ideas.

When we're talking to someone, our *voice* is the main instrument of communication: but use it sparingly.

We can nearly always afford to say less than we do. A one-page letter can convey a lot and it takes no more than a few minutes to read. Often in a half-hour's conversation we convey no more than a one-page letter ... but use a lot more words. It's sensible to find your own way in this. But the next time you're having a very important discussion, experiment by saying less than you would normally. You may find it goes a lot better, because it's not how much we say, but *what* and *how* we say it that carries people with us.

Rhythm and speed of talking should always relate to the situation and to the other person's awareness of what you are talking about. If you talk too slowly with a steady unvarying rhythm about something lightweight, it will seem pompous. If you go too fast about something that needs consideration, it will sound like oversell.

If you're not sure of your ground, decide in advance – before an important conversation – the speed at which you will talk. On music scores a composer usually gives an indication of the tempo the mood requires. It's the same when we are talking. The English language, with its mixed vowels and diphthongs, can so easily lead to a flat unexpressive way of speaking. Listen to people speaking Italian, with those open vowels at the end of words – even if you don't know the language, they always sound vital and animated.

We have to work hard to get the same effect with English. We have to work to put enthusiasm into our voice. But just as we can encourage ourselves to walk with a spring in our step which suggests vitality and purpose, we can put those same qualities into our voice. The next time you say 'Good morning' to someone, add an imaginary exclamation mark: 'Good morning!'

Public speaking and performing at sales presentations both entail different techniques from a one-to-one discussion or a meeting of half-a-dozen or so people; and there are doorstopper manuals to tell us about eye-contact and all the other public-speaking skills.

But there are ways of managing our language, which, at its best, can be wonderfully expressive and subtle: what matters is the *commitment* in the words by whoever is expressing them. At whatever stage we are, I do believe we could all do better – open up and dare a little more.

Esther Salaman, *Unlocking Your Voice*

I once attended a major presentation to chief executives of a company's clients, at which the executive in charge seemed to get everything right. He had given the presentation many times before, his eye-contact was impeccable, his stance confident, his smile unshakeable, his synchronisation with slides on TV monitors not a whisker out of place. Yet when it was all over the woman next to me said 'All that has just left me cold. What about you?' I agreed with her. The presenter had got everything right and had performed like a superbly functioning voice synchroniser. But he had missed out the most important thing: he did not *relate* to us as *people*.

Esther Salaman, a great teacher of singing, encourages her students to have 'a sense of pleasure at *being there* and sharing a performance'. Techniques of public speaking and of sales presentations are important and should be learned by anyone who has to function in this way. But nothing is as important as letting your audience feel you are sharing something with them, that you acknowledge them as individuals, not as a sea of faces with whom to make statutory *eye-contact*.

Our word 'communicate' derives from the Latin *communicare* meaning *to give* or *to share* – and this is what talking to people is all about.

REVIEW OF COMMUNICATION SKILLS

1. Remember the 'Talk to me about *me!*' principle and present your case so that it relates to the other person. This opens the door to an agreement, a sale or a contract.

2. Never be so committed to what you have decided to say that you cannot *change the script*. Every encounter brings with it the need to improvise.

3. At discussions or meetings, imagine yourself in a TV control room, cutting to close-ups of the other people. This helps to focus on *reactions* – there's no better guide to what to say next and how to say it.

4. A communication does not exist as absolute and meaningful in its own right. It is subject to the law of relativity: it's always relative to the person at the receiving end.

5. Be on guard against projecting on to someone *your* image of them. Clear away your own illusions, prejudices and fears and the way is more open for you to talk to the real person. You may know a lot about someone – but there is much more that you don't know.

6. When antagonism looms up, ask a reasonable question, rather than make a confrontational statement. If you manoeuvre someone into a corner, the only way out for them is to *fight*. A question allows a person room to manoeuvre and keeps the door open to an agreement.

7. Work at observing how body language, facial expressions, hand movements, tone of voice convey mood. This gives you greater freedom in the way you communicate, and extends your understanding of others. It is the basis of the new communication skill, *neuro-linguistic programming*.

8. Next time you are having an important discussion, try deliberately saying less than you would normally. You may find it goes a lot better!

9. Let the rhythm and speed of talking relate to the situation. Never talk too fast about something that needs consideration: it will seem like oversell.

10. Nothing is as important as making your audience feel you are sharing something with them. Our word 'communicate' derives from the Latin *communicare*, meaning *to give* or *to share*.

11. Write down straightaway one specific opportunity you expect to come up tomorrow when you can use a new technique, a new piece of knowledge, a new understanding you have read about in this chapter.

7 Communication Between Women and Men ... and the Other Way Round

How man-to-woman is different from man-to-man
How women and men can understand more about each other
How women can make their voices more resonant and authoritative
How men can rethink their working relationships with women
How to open up new creative possibilities between women and men in life, in love and at work

Whether you're a woman or a man, something like this may happen to you from time to time. Suppose you're the sales manager of a company and you receive an enquiry from a prospective customer. It looks like a big order, so you're keen and quick off the mark. The letter to you is signed:

> P R James
> Production Director

You telephone, give your name and ask for the production director. A woman answers.

'Good morning!' you say brightly, 'Is that Mr James's secretary?' There's a pause.

'No,' she replies, 'This is Philippa James speaking.' If you're a woman, you're probably pleased.

'Oh hello!' you say, 'I'm phoning about your letter.' And you get down to business. If you're a man, you might be a little put out:

'Oh, um . . .' you begin, not quite sure whether you should apologise or not.

In business and management colleges in Europe, the number of women students is edging up to 50%: a *Women in Europe* survey shows women are responsible for setting up at least one in four new businesses. By the end of the 1980s, a newspaper headline told us there are more and more . . .

WOMEN KNOCKING AT BOARDROOM DOORS

In the 1990s, forecasts indicate that *80%* of new jobs in Britain will be filled by women. Women pilots in the RAF are taking part in search and rescue operations, flying helicopters low down over the hostile North Sea. The Harley Centre for Forecasting predicts that, by the end of the century, women will make up *over half* the workforce in Britain. In the United States, the percentages of women lawyers and architects have *quintupled* in two decades, half of all accountants are now women and so are more than 25% of Wall Street high-flyers. As each year passes, the balance is shifting away from men towards their wives or girlfriends, their daughters and sisters.

To be a leader in business today, it is no longer an advantage to have been socialised as a male.

John Naisbitt & Patricia Aburdene,
Megatrends 2000

It used to be said that work for a man is his mistress, but work for a woman is never her lover. For many women that idea is as out of date as bloomers, as in the 1990s women can be just as ambitious in their careers as men are – they often get into the office earlier and stay on later.

Everyone has to fight hard to get to the top but many women feel they have to fight harder still. It has been said that if Margaret Thatcher had gone into business rather than politics, there would have been little chance of her finding her way on to the main board of one of Britain's top companies and – at least according to statistics – no chance at all of becoming chief executive. As the 1980s ended, a survey, *Women in Management in Great Britain*, revealed only eight women as directors of the UK's top hundred companies and not one woman as the boss.

This will change, because as women accept they have to be more determined, it will give them an advantage. Although you might have been surprised that the production director 'P R James' turned out to be Philippa James, the traditional perception of women as secretaries or assistants, although lingering on, is fading. The demand for managers is expected to double during the 1990s and many more women will be in line management. It is becoming commonplace for women in business and industry to be talking to men on equal terms, and often to men as their subordinates. More women are poised and determined to break through the so-called 'glass ceiling', the invisible, not-spoken-about barrier between women and most of the top jobs.

How should men and women communicate with each other at all levels in business? Is woman-to-man different from man-to-man or woman-to-woman? And how do women and men learn to understand these differences, recognise them and *use* them to make communication more productive?

When we clear up some of the mysteries and misunderstandings, we open the way to new and genuinely creative relationships between women and men in life, in love and at work. The communication skills described in this chapter have been made available through the generous help I have received from women who have talked so openly about their experiences and understanding. For it is becoming more and more evident to psychotherapists and sexologists that difficulties experienced between men and women, in bed and in the boardroom, derive from the same misunderstandings about the way each sex functions and relates.

I was discussing with three men how they interact with women. One was an 80-year-old psychiatrist, who studied in Germany and France as well as in Britain; the second was his son-in-law, a doctor in charge of a successful practice in the north of England; the third man was the doctor's son, a medical student in his final year at Cambridge.

I asked the psychiatrist whether it made much difference

if he were dealing with a man or a woman patient. He answered without hesitation: 'It's impossible to forget it's a woman.'

He was surprisingly emphatic for someone who had so clearly come to terms with the tensions and stresses most of us are still struggling with.

'What do you mean?' I asked.

'The moment a woman came into my consulting room there was a change of attitude, whether I liked it or not, and I found I was saying things in a different way.'

'Do you mean you were slightly condescending?'

'I hope not, though I expect something like that might have crept in at times. But I was aware of putting things in a gentler way. Even my voice seemed different. And I expect I smiled a bit more!' I turned to the doctor from the north of England.

'How do you see it?'

'It always makes a difference if it's a woman patient. If she's an attractive woman, there seems to be a release of extra energy. And I cheer up no end!'

'Can you say how that shows itself?'

'I might turn round in my chair more to face her and I think I smile more, too. Perhaps I'm less matter-of-fact – I'd be more likely to put a hand on her shoulder to comfort or reassure her.'

'Do those things matter all that much?'

'I think they're significant because I'm using my experience, unconsciously maybe, to deal with a woman in a different way than I deal with a man.'

I looked across at the medical student.

'What do you think?'

'I can't explain it,' he answered, 'But it's always different when I'm talking to a woman. I even imagine there's a chemical change in me and I really don't think that's exaggerating. I can sense something going on – perhaps it's a kind of biological imperative.'

Men and women are more different from each other than most people imagine or are usually prepared to admit. It's obvious their bodies are different. A biologist will tell you the very composition of their blood is different, that a man's blood is thicker and redder, with 20% more red corpuscles. A neurologist will confirm their brains develop in different ways, that the left side of the female brain develops earlier, so girls read and process information better than boys of the same age. It is not by chance that women are beginning to dominate the information technology scene. A psychiatrist will suggest men and women experience life differently, that not only are men's skins physically thicker than women's, but that men are 'thick-skinned' – they tend to be less sensitive to other people's feelings than women are.

Women, for their part, experience a unique problem, once a taboo subject: many of them are physically and psychologically off-balance for a few days every month during a large part of their lives. If they *are* aware of it all, most men find it embarrassing to talk about menstruation, although it can play a significant part in their relationships with the women in their lives. Psychotherapists believe that, even in the 1990s, few men understand this or take it into account.

None of this indicates that men are better than women, or the other way round, but there are differences which often make it difficult for one sex to understand the other. They may live together, work together, love each other, fight one another, all without really getting to know each other, except in an extraordinarily limited way. Both men and women have layers of camouflage – men, it is believed, more than women.

When we peel back some of these layers, it becomes easier for women and men to enjoy each other more freely, to understand the differences between them and to use those differences creatively. Men can be more open to placing a high value on women's sensitivity: women can allow men to express a masculine role and at the same time be aware of how that role is changing.

So what do I like about men and why do I enjoy their company? The things I particularly like about them are their *differentness*, their simplicity, their cleverness, their ability to amuse and re-tell life better than it is . . . their dependence on women . . .

Anna Ford, *Men*
Weidenfeld and Nicolson

In all this how can we leave out sex? This is a book on communication and sex, when it flows freely and is part of an emotional exchange, is the most powerful and intimate form of communication we can ever experience. The anthropologist Desmond Morris believes that '. . . to describe the human species as the *sexiest of all the primates* is not a comment on modern styles of love-making, it's a comment on the basic biological nature of the human animal'.

Sex, or the *biological imperative* as the young medical student called it, is all around us. When the student registered a 'chemical change' as he was talking to an attractive woman, he observed a fact of life. A man and a woman may be talking about business, delivery dates or profit margins, but their nervous systems may be registering sexual vibrations. James Watson, who won the Nobel Prize, admitted to hiring pretty girls to work in the Harvard laboratory, giving as a disarming reason: 'You will stay in the lab if there are pretty girls working for you . . .'

Women, as well as men, can use the current of life-force that flows between opposite poles of sexuality, to generate energy and creativity. When men and women work well together, the atmosphere can be more relaxed, more productive and more stimulating. The way women dress, their freedom to choose a wider range of colours, to use clothes to underline their femininity or their sexuality can bring a new dynamism into the workplace.

Jane Barkey, an account supervisor with the distinguished advertising agency, Ogilvy and Mather, put it in a way that echoes the view of James Watson, the Nobel prizewinner: 'Women and men can joke together more. It can be more creative – and more fun. After all, when you enjoy what you're doing, you usually end up doing it better.'

How much has changed in the 1990s, when the sexes are on an equal footing, working together to win orders or speed up the production line? There *are* changes: women can be more in charge of the situation at work and when they are exposed to sexual pressures, some are fighting back. One senior executive hangs framed prints of naked men in her elegant office, calling it a bit of 'reverse sexual harassment'. Perhaps men should not resent this counterattack because many women, even at management level, are subjected to unwelcome physical advances. A survey conducted in 1989 by The London School of Economics suggests that sexual harassment affects one in five professional women. *Newsweek* called it 'the boss's dirty little fringe benefit'.

Most men, of course, don't take advantage of their encounters with women at work and often feel the whole business is exaggerated. Evidence shows that it isn't and it's helpful if men are sensitive and aware that sexual harassment *is* a reality that constitutes a fear for more women than they realise.

To most women, male sexology is a mystery. Why do the people who run this planet behave like aliens from another as soon as they see a skirt?

Kate Saunders,
The Sunday Times, 7 May 1989

It's not all one-sided and as we move further into the 1990s the new equality is making life more difficult for men. They are being judged by new yardsticks and many of these now are women's evaluations. In bed, women are expecting equal sexual enjoyment and are not prepared any more to 'lie back and think of England'. At work, women are expecting their male colleagues to have more intuition and to be more sensitive to others; women are competing for salary increases and for more of the top jobs. Almost one in three marriages are ending in divorce and many more men are left on their own, aware they have to offer more to attract new partners. Women not only want more for themselves, they expect more from men. One by-product is that sales of men's colognes have soared!

The scene is changing. Male and female roles are at the crossroads. Some of the new skills in communication are concerned with how men and women can get the best out of each other and do their best for each other. At some management courses, men are encouraged to rethink their working relationships with women – to look not merely at what they *say* about women being equally efficient and effective, but at their underlying attitudes, conditioned maybe by years of habit and prejudice. Even in the 1990s, it's said that royal women in Britain are judged on how they dress, whereas with royal men, it depends more on what they say.

Men are being advised to listen to their voices when they are talking to women at work, to their secretary or the telephone operator or their boss, if it's a woman. What should they listen for? When women are asked about this, the word that comes up most is *condescension*. If as a man you think you're not like that, check it for yourself: *listen to your voice* when you are speaking to a woman. If you hear yourself explaining something a little too clearly, or not bothering to explain it at all, or sweeping aside objections without really considering them, you may still be playing the old game, even if you're not aware of it.

Every man has learned the trick now of using a quasi-feminist terminology. But it's not sufficient to change the language. It's like in politics – you shift the language in order to occupy the same ground.

Dennis Potter, playwright

Women, especially at secretarial or assistant levels, or as telephone operators, say how often a man will ask them to do something and tag on a diminutive such as 'sweetie', 'honey' or 'my lovely'. For every woman who 'quite likes it' there are a dozen who find it degrading. Next time you, as a man, hear yourself saying 'Would you mind doing this, dolly?' remember the odds are against you. If you want it done well and willingly, do you really want to start off by irritating the person you're asking? If you're in doubt, why not ask her how she feels about it? It could clear the air.

At assertiveness training, women are also advised to listen to their voices. What should women listen for? First of all, anything in their tone that hints at over-justifying themselves. But they are also warned against over-compensating for that tendency by being aggressive. It's not easy to get it right! Because their voices are higher in pitch, it's easier for a woman to sound more strident – Margaret Thatcher once commented about being called 'headmistressy': 'They never call a man *headmasterly*!' she complained.

Men have longer vocal cords than women so their voices

sound more forceful anyway – the nature and pitch of a woman's voice make it more difficult for her to convey authority. These are facts, not prejudices. If she wants to, it's not difficult for a woman to train herself to lower the pitch of her voice so it becomes more resonant; Margaret Thatcher worked hard to achieve this by practising humming exercises taught to her by an actor from the National Theatre.

Because humming helps to increase resonance it is a good vocal exercise for women – if you have the opportunity to be on your own before a presentation, practise humming for a while as it helps to limber up your voice. Singers often do this before going on stage.

Another technique taught to women, is simply to talk more slowly. Research shows women are inclined to talk more quickly because their feelings flow more freely – and maybe they think faster! For women, slowing down when they are putting over anything particularly important can make it sound more deliberate, more confident and more authoritative. These techniques are not to make a woman sound 'more like a man' but simply to help her have more impact. As a result, many women find they have more confidence and poise.

As for the *biological imperative* – the sexual vibes that often intrude in encounters between women and men – here is some advice offered by an attractive woman, who has built up her own business:

> Allow yourself to acknowledge the sexuality: don't pretend it's not there – but if you don't want it to get in the way, *deliberately* put it on one side, as you focus on the message you want to get across. If you hold that line firmly enough, without wavering for one moment, you will find that the men listening will take the lead from you.

This is a skill to practise, whether you're a woman or a man. But perhaps women have to be more determined.

The capacity for men and women to live together harmoniously has always affected their happiness and wellbeing: in the 1990s, their ability to work together at all levels in industry, business and the professions will have a significant effect on success in their careers. The biggest mistake is to turn your back on the situation and behave as if man-to-woman is no different from man-to-man. The truth is that both sexes need to work at understanding and respecting the differences between one another.

In spite of old hangovers, women have many things on their side. They are said to have the special ability to make coherent decisions when a number of factors must be taken into account. And when the first women astronauts were chosen, experiments showed that women could undergo much more disorientation in space than men, without being subject to nearly as much shock. Perhaps these things come more naturally to women because they are used to keeping in balance all the demands of their home, their children, their husbands coming back from the office after a dreadful day and needing love and sympathy . . . all those things, as well as their own careers.

Nor do women need to beat men 'at their own game', which was the attitude for a long time. More and more of those who are successful are learning to use their qualities as women to play the game in their own way. To get to the top by the year 2000, women must start *now* to think of themselves as potential chief executives, editors-in-chief, artistic directors, principle conductors, so they develop their own style of leadership. Before very long it will not be just a foot in the door – the doors will be wide open.

People are moving away from the concept of the manager as 'heroic leader' to that of an enabler, a problem-solver who is good at involving others in that process, and in whose style, intuition, creativity and sensitivity play important roles.

Valerie Hammond, director of research,
Ashridge Management College

In the past, men have been the universal achievers, conceiving most of the wonders of the world. As they find new partnerships with women, and learn to work with them as equals, the creative possibilities are mind-blowing. This chapter has set out a few guidelines and lit up some dark corners. There is still much more to be discovered about how men and women can cooperate in running the affairs of the world. The differences between them can be allowed to cause frustration and tension – or they can be complementary, leading to marvellous new achievements and opportunities.

REVIEW OF COMMUNICATION SKILLS

1. It's useful sometimes for men to *listen to their voices* when they're talking to women. Is there a trace of condescension? Are you explaining something a little too clearly – or not bothering to explain it at all? Are you tagging on unwelcome diminutives such as 'sweetie', 'honey' or 'dolly'? If you're not sure if she likes it, why not ask?

2. It's useful for women to listen to *their* voices, to pick up any tendency to over-justify themselves, or be more assertive or strident than the situation calls for.

3. *Humming* is a good exercise to increase resonance and authority in your voice. This can be especially useful for women, particularly before a presentation.

4. Research shows women are inclined to talk more quickly than men. Slowing down, when putting over something important, can make you sound more confident and authoritative.

5. Women must start *now* to think of themselves as potential chief executives, editors-in-chief, presidents of corporations. By the year 2000, the doors will be wide open.

6. Men can look forward to new partnerships with women, working on the same level, respecting their unique contribution. Women can allow men to express the masculine role in new and unexpected ways.

7. Man-to-woman is not the same as man-to-man or woman-to-woman. When they work at understanding the differences, men and women can get the best out of each other and do their best for each other.

8. Write down straightaway one specific opportunity you expect to come up tomorrow when you can use a new technique, a new piece of knowledge, a new understanding you have read about in this chapter.

8 Don't Just Tell Them, *Show* Them

How to develop visual communication skills
How to add dynamic impact to communication
*How to use demonstration in print, in letters, reports, brochures and
    advertisements*
How to use visual aids so they sell products and ideas
How to give visuals the immediacy of a flash of lightning

**At the annual meeting of shareholders of a company, the
president stood up to give his report.**
   'I have some good news!' he began. 'Your company's profits
have increased . . .'
He smiled, said nothing for a few moments but held up his fists,
extended the fingers of both hands and did that three times –
   '. . . *thirty* per cent!' he declared.
Everyone remembered the gesture and the percentage increase.
   What is considered to be the first real television commercial
was made in 1954. It was for a headache remedy and showed
hammers banging away at an agonised skull. The banging
stopped and the skull relaxed. The client paid $8,400 for
the commercial – but Rosser Reeves, head of the advertising
agency that produced it, claimed it made more money in sev-
en years than *Gone With the Wind* made for MGM in a quarter
of a century.
   President Bush opened his campaign against 'crack', the
cocaine alkaloid obtained from cola leaves, sitting at his desk

in the White House. Millions of TV viewers saw him pick up a small white packet which he held up to the camera:

'This looks as innocent as a box of candy,' he said. He opened the packet and tipped some white powder on to his desk.

'But it's turning our cities into battlefronts . . . It's poison.'

What do those three examples of powerful and successful communication have in common? They not only passed on the message in words, they *showed* what those words meant: take away the visual impact and the message becomes two-dimensional.

Studies show we take in 80% of all information *through our eyes*: we remember much more of what we see than what we hear. The first impression someone makes on us is what they *look* like. Our visual response to sunlight and bright colours can change our whole mood. 'Let me see. . .' we say, when we want to reflect on something. 'Seeing is believing' is a maxim as old as the hills.

Look up from this page and look across the room: register for a few moments all the impacts that are coming at you. Now close your eyes for five seconds and think how much you have cut off. When you are trying to convince, persuade, affect people, always look for ways of *showing* them, as well as telling them. If you leave that out, you are ignoring an essential unchanging truth about how the human organism processes information.

Despite all the talking and listening we do we remain essentially a visual animal. In this way we do not differ greatly from our close relatives, the monkeys and apes. The whole primate order is a vision-dominated group. . .

Desmond Morris, *Bodywatching*

When we communicate we always want to make an impact of some kind and we measure our success by how much impact we make. Every time you put into your communication a good visual component, its impact leaps up. When the president of the company opened and closed his hands three times, he was expressing *visually* 10 . . . 20 . . . 30%. When that historic TV commercial showed hammers banging away at a skull, it was *showing* the agony of a headache. When President Bush held up that small white package, he was contrasting *visually* something that looked 'as innocent as a box of candy' with the deadly menace of 'crack'.

Recall and impact tests demonstrate that the smallest visual element in a communication, even something seemingly banal, increases the response much more than we could ever imagine. If you are saying that sales are increasing, why not use your forefinger to trace the line of an imaginary sales graph going up? Everyone will remember the gesture and what it means. If you are explaining how a new system can save time, work out how many days that adds up to in a year. Tear off, one at a time, the same number of sheets from a page-a-day calendar and hold them up – or better still, as one speaker did, toss the pages of the calendar at the audience. You will make the point unforgettably.

These ideas are so simple that you may worry about 'talking down' to people. Evidence shows that even highly intelligent people respond to the most ordinary visual demonstrations. Translating words, written or spoken, into meaning and significance requires some mental effort, and a pause whilst something is expressed in simple visual terms changes the rhythm and provides an unconscious relief.

It is well known that a high proportion of intelligent individuals process information at their best in a non-verbal or a visual-spatial way. Einstein and Leonardo de Vinci, two of the greatest brains, were cases in point . . .

Peter J Congdon, director
Gifted Children's Information Centre

Words have their place and using the best words is a vital power skill in communication. Successful copywriters are sought after and paid ever higher salaries – at the same time, communication becomes more *visual* every year. People spend more and more time in front of VDUs (visual display units). Ten-year-old children write letters on wordprocessors, watching their words come up on a screen. Information technology is taking over as the primary way we communicate, and are communicated with, and a *screen* is the ever-present 'interface' between us and the message. Everyone is thinking more visually now and we must respond by increasing the visual content of communication.

How can we learn about using visual techniques to make our communications more powerful? The most up-to-date course, which cost millions of pounds and dollars to set up, is on tap for us at home: we can put our feet up and use our own television set to see the work and methods of the most highly paid communicators in the world. But it's not enough just to look at television: we must study the visual techniques it uses, with a notepad on hand.

When you look at people talking on TV, particularly at a discussion where there are two or three taking part, watch the way they use their hands and their bodies to underline points they are making. Gestures add an important visual content to something you are saying. If there are *three* points to make, count them out on your fingers. If you are talking about the impact something will make, consider thumping the table to make the point. Watch how the experts do it on television, because they have usually been through expensive courses on how to present facts and figures effectively. See what you can adapt for yourself, make a note of it and *try it out* as soon as you can.

Sometimes it's useful to turn off the sound and just watch people talking on television, which focusses your mind on visual aspects. When there are three people talking and you look at them with the sound turned off, you will nearly always find that one is more effective than the others, even though you cannot hear what is being said. It may be because they lean forward in their chair, or hold out their hands, or lift up their head. Try this exercise from time to time, looking at people on TV with the sound turned off. You will find it a constant source of new visual ideas.

Study commercials. The best ones have been worked over many times, tested in front of sample audiences and reworked to increase their effectiveness. When you see a commercial that makes you sit up and think about the product it's advertising, ask yourself how it works. What are the visual components that pull you towards it? This adds to your stock of visual ideas and you may be able to adapt some of them for yourself. But even if you can't, it will increase your awareness of the visual content of communication.

In print, for example in letters, where you don't have sound or movement, you can often add a visual aspect, even demonstrate something, by finding an idea that takes your reader into the picture. It's called *demonstration in print* and you should always look for that possibility. To get you going, here are some masterly examples:

An advertisement for the Audi 100 actually *demonstrates* how quiet it is: Dr Wimmer, head of acoustics at the Audi factory, explains:

> At 70mph, the noise in the cabin
> is just 66.5 decibels. . . to give you
> some idea how quiet that is, a
> newspaper creates approximately 72
> decibels every time you turn a page.

And the headline for the whole-page ad uses words to bring the idea to life:

> AT 70MPH, THE NEW AUDI 100
> MAKES LESS NOISE THAN YOU WILL
> TURNING THIS PAGE

The advertisement for Hitachi electric shavers found another way to demonstrate in print: here is the headline:

> THIS SHAVER'S FOIL IS THINNER THAN THIS PAGE.
> THE SHAVE IT GIVES IS AS SMOOTH.

Printing something *upside down* just to attract attention is a cheap trick and usually does nothing to convince anyone. One day an entire advertisement in *The Independent* was printed upside down. Readers dutifully turned the page round to see what it was about. This time the medium *was* the message. The simple headline, when we read it the right way up, stated:

> THE SIMPLEST
> MISTAKES
> CAN RUIN
> A SLIDE
> PRESENTATION

It continued 'There's nothing as embarrassing as a slide mounted upside down or back to tnorf'. It was an advertisement for a presentation company who double-check everything.

Preparation and production of *visual aids* for presentations, sales conferences and person-to-person selling has become big business. The message has got through and industry in the 1990s is alert to the importance of non-verbal communication. Everyone in an organisation, from the chief executive downwards, knows how important it is to use visual ways to communicate with customers – and also with the people working with and for them.

It's not enough just to include a few pictures or charts in catalogues, brochures and presentations. We have to choose illustrations and work on them so they really add force to written or spoken messages. The first test to apply is this:

Does the visual *do* something words cannot do equally well?

If the answer is *no*, look for something that turns that answer into *yes*. Look for visuals that are unexpected, that add drama and impact to what you are saying or writing. The marketing director for a car manufacturer, presenting a new model to the trade said, 'We have included a whole list of *extras* in the standard showroom price'. He could have projected a slide with the extras listed. Instead he *showed* what was on offer: he propped up a complete car door, pressed a button and the window went down. 'Electrically-operated windows!' he declared. He held up a steering column and, turning the steering wheel easily with one finger, announced: 'Power steering!' He went on like that.

When he finished his demonstrations, he asked 'Do you know how much it would cost to *buy* those as extras? He unfolded a large rectangular piece of paper and held it up between both hands. It was a giant cheque with $3000 written on it.

That presentation was a lot of trouble, as everything had to be specially prepared. But everyone went away from it remembering the message: the time and money were repaid many times over by the impact the demonstrations produced.

Millions of pounds and dollars are spent on research into visual aids. It doesn't have to be guesswork – we can often know *in advance* whether we are using visual material in the most effective way. Remember all the time that the people you are talking to will take away mental images far more readily than verbal memories and those images last much longer. Psychologists say visual memory is near-perfect: something you have seen on television can stay with you for years.

What follows are highlights of some of the most advanced research on how visual ideas make an impact, how they succeed and why they fail. The conclusions turn out to be extraordinarily simple; the human organism, complex though it is, so often responds to a direct straightforward approach. One of the most powerful TV spots ever made showed a pretty child picking daisies. The scene ended with a nuclear explosion. Viewers who saw it have never forgotten the visual and emotional impact from the juxtaposition of childhood innocence with the horrors of cataclysmic destruction.

Diagrams, tables and charts are used both in reports and brochures, and in person-to-person presentations. Research tells us the most common mistake is to make them too complicated, to pack in more information than people can take in easily, instead of keeping a sharp focus on one, two or at the most three points. Aim to make visuals communicate like a flash of lightning – if people have to work at understanding what you are showing them, the chances are you have failed.

Look at any chart or diagram you are planning to use and ask how long it takes to explain it – if the answer is more than 15 seconds, *simplify it*. Diagrams in technical journals for specialists are something else: those are not so much visual aids as technical expositions, such as engineering drawings or architects' plans, which are required to be complete and detailed. Although these are appropriate for specialist-to-specialist communication, they will usually fail when they are used for specialist-to-layman presentation.

In non-technical presentations, check the visuals you want to use for *impact* rather than exposition. Of course the two can be combined at times but impact should take the lead. Tables of figures have less impact than graphs, graphs less impact than diagrams, diagrams less impact than pictures. The whole lot put together has less impact than the real thing, the objects themselves, especially if you can use them to demonstrate how well they work. The marketing director presenting the new car used a real door, a real steering wheel and a giant cheque. If you want your visuals to work as hard as possible, push them as far along that progression – from tables of figures to the objects themselves – as you possibly can. If it's not possible to go beyond tables, at least make these simple and use different colours to animate them.

When you are walking or driving through a city, look at *posters*. A good poster has to communicate with us, even when we catch it in passing – otherwise it's a waste of money. Nobody ever stands in front of a poster trying to puzzle it out! Good posters are the ones that make us look a second time and hold our imagination; when you find out how they work, make a note of the ideas and adapt them to improve your own visuals.

A double-sheet poster for Eagle Star Insurance was entirely filled with a pane of shattered glass. Across the glass was one short statement:

> Eagle Star can get you
> a glazier, free of charge,
> 24 hours a day

Pictures and words work together and the result is you remember the one simple direct message. The medium *is* the message!

Eagle Sar used the '*close-up*' technique. There was no frame around the window: we were focussed on the shattered pane of glass and nothing else. Close-ups are more telling than general shots: if something is important to us we look *closely* at it. Close-ups on television 'bite' in a way that a more open shot can never do, especially extreme close-ups. Look for possibilities of using close-ups in your own visual aids; even with a table of figures, you can move in BIG on the *one* figure you want everyone to remember.

When you are planning visuals, look at each one and ask the same question: '*Can I make it more simple?*' Often too much cleverness, too much bland sophistication have less effect than a spontaneous approach. A thick felt pen, if you can handle it, can offer a directness and an immediacy that electrify an audience. When Sony took an expensive double-page colour advertisement to tell the world how a Sony Black Trinitron makes colour more vivid, they used 'a demonstration by Samantha, aged 5'. Samantha supplied two drawings of a flower, using the same coloured crayons: one was against a grey background, representing standard television sets: the other was against a *black* background. The colours against black looked much more vivid – a 5-year-old's drawings proved the point.

Some people feel a *blackboard*, a 'chalk-and-talk' presentation, is too back-to-school. Yet watching a presenter write on a blackboard can make a strong personal link between them and the audience; surrounded by high-tech communication, the rudimentary simplicity of a blackboard can be a welcome relief. I have seen a blackboard used effectively even for a presentation to top management: the senior executives seemed to respond and enjoy the direct way it underlined the main points of the proposition. Maybe blackboards have an association with authority which encourages us to accept them for visual exposition.

It's not easy to write clearly on a blackboard and needs practice: squeaky chalk is a distraction. Anything that gives the impression that you are not in complete control will seriously undermine your credibility. So plan the best layout in advance on a sheet of paper, which will give you confidence when you come to set it out on the blackboard itself. Where possible use telling keywords rather than sentences, and figures that summarise results rather than lead up to them.

Flip-charts are the next stage up. They have the advantage over the blackboard in that you can prepare sheets beforehand, keeping them covered up until you want to show them. Or if you are confident enough and have worked on it in rehearsals, you can hold the attention of your audience with brilliant while-they-watch visuals. Flip-charts have no technical problems, no screen, switches, bulbs, or fuses to go wrong.

John May is an international lecturer who runs advanced courses on management presentations. He advises that our 'use of a flip-chart can be as sophisticated as a Picasso or as primitive as graffiti, according to your wish, or skill and the requirements of the occasion'. He adds some life-saving advice: prepare flip-chart sheets with lightly pencilled-in horizontal and vertical guidelines and outlines of graphs or diagrams. From where they are sitting, your audience is unlikely to see the light pencil lines and will be impressed by your assurance and skill as you go over them with a felt pen! Another good suggestion is to use alternate *blank* sheets, so you can get rid of a visual just by covering it up and then uncover the next one when you're ready for it.

An *overhead projector* is as basic as a bicycle and just as familiar. What you write or draw on the light-table in front of you, is lit up and projected on the screen above and behind you. You can face your audience while you're using it and switch it on or off whenever it suits you. If you want to, you can have everything prepared professionally in advance on 250mm (10in) square transparencies – a diagram can be built up with successive overlays, drawings from books or journals can be photocopied (subject to copyright clearance if necessary) as black lines on clear acetate, which you can write on directly while they are projected.

OHPs are versatile and user-friendly, yet the effect often comes across as unsophisticated, with a hint of the magic lantern about it. This may be because they are commonplace and are not usually used for top-level presentations. You can go some way to overcoming these drawbacks by making sure the mechanics are perfectly arranged in advance, that the table is the right height with the screen high enough so the projected images are clearly visible. You can have slides superbly prepared, demonstrating that a lot of work has been done. Or you can draw or write your material *live* in front of your audience – so long as you rehearse everything so well that you come over as totally in control.

When your audience is watching a projected image, even from an OHP, they will unconsciously associate it with the cinema or television and expect the same level of professional polish: to achieve this requires preparation and practice. The overhead projector is a good standby, provided you use it with skill and imagination, in a way that relates to the situation and the people you are talking to.

Two things undermine the effectiveness of so many visual presentations: *lighting* and *legibility*. In the theatre, lighting is considered almost on a par with the design of the set: you should give it the same importance, as lighting can make a presentation look alert and vital, or make it seem downbeat. Whenever possible, visit in advance the room you are going to use to see whether the lighting can be improved: could you have a little more light on you and on what you are showing? Are there distracting reflections? Dead bulbs, even only one or two, are off-putting, so always get them replaced, even if it means making a fuss.

People may have to look at your visuals up to 10m (30ft) away or more. Make sure *you* look at them from at least the same distance. If your audience has to strain to see anything, this will take too much effort and they will soon give up. When you are using words or figures, make them big enough; single out the ones that really matter and make those *twice as big*.

If you are talking to only a few people, or even to just one person, no visual aid is as effective as the real thing. Nothing involves anyone more than giving them something to handle and operate for themselves. An ancient Chinese proverb teaches: 'I hear and forget. I see and remember. I do and I am convinced'. If that was Confucius, he would have made a brilliant presenter and a great salesman. If there is any possibility, always look for a way of letting people try something for themselves: 'I do and I am convinced' is not far away from *I do and I buy!*

Whether you use a blackboard, flip-charts, a projector or demonstrate with the real thing, the guiding principle is to use them sparingly. Too many visuals, no matter how good, can turn a talk into a 'fun and games' show and can give the impression you're afraid to speak about something without constant visual props. The more serious the message you have to get across, the more sparing you should be with visual aids. Use them for *underlining* a point, to add *drama* or for a *change of pace* – but not so often that the medium gets in the way of the message.

Using visual aids is like putting on a one-man or a one-woman show. And shows have to be rehearsed. Timing is vital, and timing can only be worked out in rehearsal. Even turning the sheets of a flip-chart can be done with confidence and authority – or awkwardly, as if you're not quite sure what's going to happen next.

As well as the presenter of the spoken word, you are now a conjurer, a juggler and a showman. See that the visuals work for you, not you for them.

John May, *How to Make Effective Business Presentations*

In the end when you are talking to people, *you* should be in charge and if you don't come across that way, you will never convince others. Make sure you look at your audience and talk to *them* – not to a slide, a flip-chart or a blackboard. And when you have finished with a visual, cover it up or get rid of it, so that there's nothing to distract people from what *you* are telling them. The best advice given at courses on business presentations is this: 'Think of *yourself* as your *number one* visual aid'. That will encourage your audience to see you in the same way.

REVIEW OF COMMUNICATION SKILLS

1. When you are trying to convince, persuade, affect others, look for ways of *showing* them, as well as telling them. Every time you inject a good visual component, impact leaps up.

2. Never worry about using simple visual ideas because of the risk of 'talking down' to people. It is believed even Einstein and Leonardo da Vinci responded more readily to images than words.

3. Remember in the 1990s everyone is used to *looking*: a *screen* is the 'interface' between us and information technology. To keep pace, we must increase the visual content of our communications.

4. Study *television*, notepad in hand. Look at discussions on TV and see how people use their hands and their bodies to underline points. Turn off the sound occasionally and watch people talking, so you focus on *visual* techniques. See what you can adapt for yourself, make a note of it and *try it out*.

5. Study *TV commercials*: the best ones have been worked over many times to increase their effectiveness. Make a note of any visual ideas you can adapt.

6. Use *demonstration in print* whenever you can. Look for ways in letters or reports to make an idea tangible and dramatic, even by using the paper it's written on.

7. Apply this test to visual aids:
Does it do something that
words cannot do equally well?
If the answer is *no*, look for something that will change that answer to *yes*. It may cost more money and take more time,

but this will be repaid many times over in impact and sales.

8. Look at any chart or diagram or table you are planning to use and ask how long it takes to explain: if the answer is more than 15 seconds, *simplify it*. Aim to give visuals the immediacy of a flash of lightning!

9. Study good *posters*, the ones that make you look a second time, the ones that interest you in what they're selling. Work out how they make such an *immediate* impact: nobody ever stops in front of a poster to puzzle it out!

10. Use *close-ups* for maximum impact. Move in BIG on the one figure, the one image, the one phrase you want everyone to remember.

11. Use visual aids to *underline* a point, to add *drama* or for a *change of pace*. But not so often that the medium gets in the way of the message.

12. Think of *yourself* as your *number one* visual aid. That will encourage your audience to see you in the same way.

13. Write down straightaway one specific opportunity you expect to come up tomorrow when you can use a new technique, a new piece of knowledge, a new understanding you have read about in this chapter.

9 Phone Power

How to relate to the telephone in the 1990s, making it a natural
*   extension of yourself*
How to 'draft' an important phone call, before you make it
How to increase confidence, authority and assertiveness on the phone
How to listen actively instead of passively
How to bring the new phone power skills into your life and work

**By the time you finish reading this chapter, a telephone
will not be an inert plastic box of microchips and transis-
tors that can make you uncertain or apprehensive when it
rings.** It will be transformed into a lifeline that relates you to
other people, enables you to get things done, help others and
sell goods and ideas. You will pick it up to take a call or tap
out a number, using it like a technological slave ready to do
what *you* want it to.

This is the era of the phone. Business communications
are dominated by it. The telephone networks of the world
are the new marketplace, the new forum to meet people and
to buy and sell goods and services. Telephones have become
much more than a means of interconnecting one person with
another: the *phonezone* has brought the whole world almost
instantly to our desks, or in fact to *anywhere* we happen to
be. For phones are now for people, rather than for places.
In Britain, it is scheduled that portable phones will be in the
hands of 15 million people by the end of the century, with a
market of £7 billion a year. These portable phones will be
cheap, lightweight and more reliable than the cellular handsets

of the 1980s and wherever we are they will keep us in touch 24 hours a day.

Teleworkers will make up a big percentage of the workforce of the industrial world; they will be freed from time and geographical restraints, *telecommuting* – going to work by reaching out to pick up a phone. The saving in costs will be staggering, as it's estimated that city-centre based workers cost *three times* their actual salaries in rents and overheads (the figure quoted by Rank Xerox for central London). Teleworking will increase the world's workforce, since it will bring in mothers with small children – women willing and able to use specialised skills working from home.

Telemarketing increases the number of a salesman's client contacts in a day from maybe half-a-dozen or so to thirty or more, with the cost of each contact cut to a fraction of what it used to be. Telemarketing allows individual members of a salesforce to be instantly integrated into a national campaign, with hour by hour supervision by a sales manager and a continuous hotline link to production.

Once you develop the techniques for getting through to the right people, telephoning becomes cost-effective because of the sheer volume.

Norman Bate, managing director,
Roche Audio Visual
(British Telecom case study)

Cars will become mobile working centres. Some executives are already asking 'With a car like this, who needs an office?' From their cars they are dictating letters and reports to wordprocessing units, sending facsimile documents and plans, tapping into mainframe computers and using the carphone to make the majority of their person-to-person contacts with clients and their staff.

Digital systems will improve the quality of telephone communication, giving it the same presence as talking face-to-face. Healthcall, which operates a *dial-up docs* service, is demonstrating this, offering recorded medical advice by phone on sexual problems, premenstrual tension, depression, Aids and a whole range of other health problems, for which people would normally visit their doctor or local health centre.

The telephone is cutting across the traditional nine-to-six daily pattern and some executives are paying a price for the constant availability the phone brings into their lives. Peter Parker, former chairman of British Rail, complained 'I sometimes feel imprisoned, electronically tagged'. Other executives complain of backache, headache and tenseness, all symptoms of stress taking over. When you learn to relate to the telephone as a natural extension of yourself, using the skills in this chapter, stress and tension come under control: the new phone power skills help you to become master of the telephone instead of its victim.

Let's start by making a telephone call. We are talking about an important call, of course, not a quick routine call to find out something or make a simple arrangement. Suppose the call you are about to make could lead to a big order, open up an important new contact, comfort or reassure someone in distress, or play a significant role in a personal relationship. However nervous you may be, the fact that *you* are making the call gives you an advantage. *You* are taking the initiative, *you* are in the driving seat, at least to begin with – and will be throughout the call, when you have learnt the skills. You have an unparalleled head start: you know why you are making the call, what you want from it, you can make notes in advance and refer to them, without the other person seeing you. All that is thrown away if you just pick up the phone without preparing for the conversation to come.

This preparation starts with a piece of A4 paper. At the top you write what you want to accomplish by your phone call, a clear statement of objectives. You then know the essential points to make, and could even write a few phrases that will help to make them in a more telling way. Prepare for both a *yes* or a *no* response, so you are not put out by either. If you are faced with a rejection, even a curt one, *smile* and say 'Thank you for listening'. That leaves you in control and will help to counter a let-down feeling that could affect the rest of your day.

Have everything you might need ready to hand. If you are positive and know what you're about, the person you are calling is likely to take their cue from you. When you want to make an appointment, have alternative dates ready, so there's no fumbling or hesitation. Telemarketers write out a sales script in advance and they will work at this as hard as they would at an important sales letter. At the bottom of your A4 paper write down the last message you want to leave with the person you're calling, even the actual words you might say.

When you are satisfied with your preparation notes, you are almost ready to make the call. But not quite. Before actors go on stage, they prepare for their entrance: they get in the right mood and sometimes do vocal exercises in the wings. If the phone call is important enough to warrant it, you can do that. Three long deep breaths before you pick up the phone will help you to be alert. Swinging your arms will relax the shoulders and the neck where tension usually starts. If all this seems like overkill, is it any different from drafting an important letter and going over it carefully two or three times before the final version is sent? A telephone call can be just as important.

Many people make crucial calls with far less preparation than for a person-to-person meeting. Yet a telephone call *is* a person-to-person meeting: it may be casual or routine, or it may have the potential to change your whole life. How often have you made a phone call and ended it, only to realise a few minutes later there were some important points you should have made . . . and didn't? If you work on it beforehand and *write down* everything you want to cover, you can tick off points as you go along. Once you have tried this, and see for yourself how effective it can be and how much it can reduce stress and tension, it will become a standard part of your 'phone power'.

Making notes in advance also helps you to learn a great deal about management of *time* on the telephone. Studies show that most phone calls are on average 50% longer, or even more, than is necessary to achieve their purpose: there is not sufficient focus on the aim of the call. Brief notes made in advance may help you to save an hour or two a day, up to 10–20% of your working time. Using the telephone economically, in terms of time, makes a big contribution to our output, and people you are speaking to will respect you for not taking up more of *their* time than is necessary. And it all starts with 'drafting' a telephone call in advance.

Receiving a phone call is a different situation. Generally, we have to cope without preparation, although sometimes, when we know the call is especially important, there's the possibility of asking 'May I call you back in ten minutes?' That gives us the chance to make a few quick notes, get into the driving seat and make the call ourself. When this is not possible or advisable, what can you do?

You can *stand up*: this always increases concentration and can add authority to your tone of voice. It makes a difference even to push yourself into sitting up straight. You can clench your fist hard and then relax your hand – this builds up assertiveness and is an exercise taught to actors to prepare for a positive entrance on stage. We are psycho-physical organisms: what we do with our bodies affects our mental state, which is revealed in our voice and which in turn affects the person listening. If you slump in a chair or cross your legs, your diaphragm is constricted and your voice will often sound less resonant and positive. On the phone, your voice is the only part of you that counts, so give it every help you can and it will reward you by being more convincing, more responsive and more effective.

We have been looking at things that affect the impact *you* make. But a telephone call is *two-way*. Whatever you are doing at the time, whatever is going on in your day, whatever is on your mind, the most important thing – if you want a conversation to go well – is to make a positive effort to focus on the other person for those few minutes you are talking to them. Above all, *listen*. Listening is so important in communicating that there's a special chapter about it further on in this book. On the phone, distinguish between passive listening and *active* listening: you cannot see the other person and the only guide you have to what they really mean and how they feel is what they are saying – and how they are saying it.

Most people listen passively, the way we breathe – the words simply flow over them. *Active* listening is caring about what the other person is saying, focussing on the words they are using and switching on to their tone of voice. It has been likened to walking: sometimes we simply go for a stroll, with no particular destination in mind. At other times – when we are walking to the station for example, and have to get there on time – our walking is directed and purposeful. *Active listening* is like that: directed towards understanding what the other person means, purposeful in the aim to make the conversation succeed.

Do you *doodle* while you're on the phone, draw squiggles

or construct abstract designs? Many people do this because they're nervous – it's similar to fidgeting. If it is one of your habits, try to stop it, as it diverts attention and your response to the person you're talking to can become mechanical. Another reason is that far from helping to relieve nervousness, we're told it's counterproductive, as it in fact makes us even more tense.

Lesley Bremness, the writer and expert on herbs, offers an alternative. Keep a bowl of dried lavender by the telephone, she recommends, and let the flowers run through your fingers: as the aroma wafts up, it has a calming effect. It's been known for centuries that herbs have medicinal and therapeutic properties, and if telephone tension is one of your problems, it's worth following up her suggestion. It has certainly worked effectively for some people, even people at the top exposed to the intense pressure of having to make immediate far-reaching decisions.

Good listening on the telephone is giving someone time to explain why they have phoned, and time to say what they want, while you wait your turn without interrupting, until you are sure you have all the facts. If you think you already do that, listen to yourself next time someone phones you; you may find you jump in on them sooner than you realise. That's the usual pattern, because our mind is racing ahead to what *we* want to say.

When we speak too soon we miss out on a valuable opportunity. Waiting until the other person has said everything they want to, not only gives the impression we are treating them as important (which we are), it gives us time to plan what we want to say. We can even pull a pad towards us and make notes, so when the time comes for us to respond, we are prepared. 'Phone power' makes full use of our 'invisibility' to the other person!

Some phone power skills derive directly from neurology and psychology. They take into account the way the brain – that mass of nervous tissue within your skull – is divided into two cerebral hemispheres, linked by a tract of fibres to your nervous system. These hemispheres have different functions, controlling not only different sides of the body but different psychological reactions. If you want to clench your *right* hand, it's the opposite side of your brain, the *left* side, that transmits the neuro-message. The left hemisphere also controls speech and the way we handle words; it is the part of the brain that processes information, works things out logically and enables us to make decisions based on understanding the facts.

The right side of the brain has a less tangible function and it has taken longer for neurologists to understand it. As far as we know, the right cerebral hemisphere relates to imagination, intuition and creative ideas. It enables us to arrive at a solution to a problem without knowing logically how we got there. When we 'jump to a conclusion' and it turns out to be more reliable in the long run than one we have painstakingly worked out, it's the right side of the brain we have to thank. It is also believed this side of the brain enables us to respond with sensitivity and understanding to another person.

We can use this knowledge to add to our phone power. Our *right* ear, like our right hand, is linked to the *left* cerebral hemisphere, the *left* ear to the *right* hemisphere. On the phone, we don't usually think about which ear we listen with but it could make a marked difference to how we handle the conversation. Proof is difficult to establish. Neurologists and psychologists believe there is probably something in it, but hesitate to go further. Yet those people who deliberately choose which ear to listen with, according to the circumstances, have found it changes their whole approach to using the telephone.

If you are dealing with complex information, discussing budgets or estimates or investments, it makes sense to listen with your *right* ear. This will connect more readily to the left side of the brain, the side that reasons for us and analyses data. If it's a conversation when you want to be more intuitive, find a brilliant solution to a problem, or be more compassionate and more understanding, try listening with the *left* ear. That is the direct line to the right side of the brain, the source of our sensitivity and creativity.

It must be added that it's not easy to change from the ear you usually listen with, and it may feel uncomfortable to begin with. But the experiment is recommended. Even try switching from one ear to another in the middle of a conversation, another way of making use of your 'invisibility' on the telephone. If you become aware of differences in the way you process and deal with information, you should develop the habit of choosing which ear to listen with. If you're discussing anything to do with money, it could save you an expensive mistake!

When you are on the phone, you may think the expressions on your face do not matter, because the other person can't see them. But our expressions can change our mood and our *voice* will transmit that over the telephone. There's evidence that *smiling* has a neurological effect on us, activating encephalins – compounds found in parts of the brain and spinal cord – that have a direct effect on our mood, making us more upbeat and vital. If things are going wrong and you are trying to put them right with a phone call, try smiling as you tap out the number: the confident mood that results can help you get a better response. If you *stand up* and smile, it's even more effective. Standing up makes us take in more air, makes our heart beat a little faster and the result is more energy and vitality when we start speaking.

Stanislavsky, the innovative Russian theatre director, taught how *gesture* can be used to bring on a state of mind that enables actors to identify with the characters they are playing. The Actors' Studio in New York developed these ideas into 'method' acting, which gave the performances of actors such as Marlon Brando and Rod Steiger a new depth and power. Speaking on the telephone, we have to convey authority, decisiveness, determination, sympathy, reassurance – with our *voice*, and it is not far-fetched to use some of the ideas taught at the Actors' Studio.

If you can overcome your inhibitions, try 'acting' a little when you're on the phone and you're far more likely to come over as a living vital presence to the other person. They will become more involved, and more likely to respond to what you are offering them or what you're asking them to do. It is not only the words you use, but how you say them. Take the simple greeting, 'Hello': it can sound indifferent or even resentful, welcoming and inviting, even loving. The ordinary word 'yes' said in different ways can convey a whole spectrum of meanings from doubt and suspicion to total support.

In the theatre, someone can say 'yes' in such a way that the 'yes' is no longer ordinary – it can become a beautiful word, because it is the perfect expression of what cannot be expressed in any other way.

Peter Brook, *The Shifting Point*

Clenching your fist tightly two or three times helps to add a firm edge to your voice. If you want to come over as helpful and cooperative, stretch out an arm with the palm turned upwards, fingers extended: your voice will tend to soften. If you have a 'hands-free' loudspeaking phone, you can be more expansive with gestures and use both hands, another way of taking advantage of your 'invisibility'.

Until you get used to the idea, you may feel awkward trying these suggestions. People who teach such techniques advise us to listen to our voice. As we hear it sounding more authoritative, more confident or more understanding, we learn the value of the gestures and movements that bring out those qualities.

Good communication on the phone relates directly to the person at the other end of the line, just as a good performance in the theatre relates to the audience. With practice you can train yourself to get *instant telephone vibes*: you tune into the kind of person you are talking to, or if it's someone you know, into the mood they are in. The most successful telesales people, making fifty or more calls a day, have learnt to develop an instant feeling, as the other person answers, about how to proceed.

If the telephone is the primary way you contact people, you can develop the same awareness by *listening* more actively. When people phone you, it's as if they are coming through your door – and what do you do when someone comes to see you? You look at them: you see whether they're nervous, tired, under pressure, or relaxed. And if you listen in the right way on the phone, it's almost the same as looking at someone. You have to work at this and always remember that 'invisibility' operates at *both* ends of the line.

With practice, you can penetrate telephone invisibility by listening to voices as you look at faces: one of the first signs of depression, for example, is a falling-off of the voice, a loss of resonance as the vocal cords go flabby, the way depressed people slump in a chair. You can hear this, just as you can hear and recognise other moods. The next time you make a phone call, *tune in* for a few moments and pick up attraction, unwillingness, warmth, fear or whatever other feeling is coming over the line. It's useful to *picture* the other person talking to you, particularly if you know them. And as you work at this, it's surprising how visual a telephone call can be.

Any technique that makes the person at the other end less disembodied makes a telephone conversation more direct and more productive.

The telephone is the medium most commonly used for making complaints and *any* complaint exposes you to the risk of losing a customer. People making complaints are usually angry, or nervous, or apprehensive: if you listen and let them talk out their feelings, resisting the temptation to stop them in mid-flow, you will already have gone a long way towards making them feel better. Psychotherapists acknowledge they do more good by *listening* than by talking.

The telephone now plays the major role in customer or client service and is often the deciding factor in whether a business is successful or not. This has led to more training courses on how to use the telephone. The same key points always emerge: no matter how busy you are, never sound impatient as it will leave the other person feeling unwanted – not the way you'd want any customer to feel. Aim to make customers *enjoy* talking to you.

Proctor and Proctor, one of the top telemarketing agencies, coined the acronym MIETSY for dealing with customers. MIETSY means *make it easy to say yes*. Like many sales techniques it may sound glib or simplistic. But when we pick up the phone, it is often because we want to make something happen – which means we want someone to *do* something. MIETSY is a good guide to how to go about it. The customer service section of British Airways uses the MIETSY approach and have found it 'an uplifting experience that can only lead to doing more business through better performance'.

When we arrange to see someone, we usually make an appointment: they are expecting us and have set aside the time. When we telephone them, we are going in without even knocking on the door. In certain cases, depending on who they are, it's worth asking whether they're free to talk for a few minutes. If not, you can make an appointment to call them back at an agreed time. At the worst they may say they've only got a couple of minutes to spare, so at least you know from the outset how long *you've* got.

> As the conversation proceeds, voices tell whether they wish you'd get the hell off the phone and not prolong anything or it's going okay. You cannot fail to get signals without even asking, so listen and do what the signals say.
>
> Helen Gurley Brown, *Having It All*

Never lie about why you are phoning, as it usually arouses suspicion and resentment. Do not, that is, talk about all manner of other things, and then say 'Oh, by the way, do you think you could . . .' No-one is fooled by this and it shows you're unsure of yourself. You probably know people who do this all the time, and while they're talking about the weather, their holiday or whatever, you are thinking 'I wonder what they *really* want!' It's always better to come out in the open right from the start and tell the other person why you are phoning.

At one course on phone power, a large notice behind the lecturer asks:

DO YOU LOOK YOUR BEST ON THE PHONE?

When we go to see someone whose decision is important to us, we take the trouble to look our best. On the phone people will, consciously or unconsciously, form a mental image of you and will 'see' far more than you realise. Treat an important telephone call with the same respect as you would an important face-to-face interview: straighten your tie or your dress and even comb your hair – if that makes you feel better!

REVIEW OF COMMUNICATION SKILLS

1. Before making an important telephone call, write down what you want the call to accomplish, a clear statement of objectives. Add a few phrases that will help make your points. Then write the last thought you want to leave with the person you're calling, even the words you might say.

2. Have everything you might need ready to hand, including alternative dates if you want to make an appointment, so there's no fumbling or hesitation. When you are positive, the person at the other end will take their cue from you.

3. If it's an important call, take three long deep breaths before you pick up the phone. That will make you more alert. Swing your arms to relax your shoulders and neck where tension usually starts.

4. Treat a telephone call with the same respect as you would a person-to-person meeting, because that is exactly what it is.

5. Use brief notes made in advance to help you manage telephone time more efficiently. Studies show you could save 50%, or even more, of the time used on phone calls, which adds 10/20% to your working day, almost one extra day a week!

6. If an important phone call catches you unprepared, consider asking 'May I call you back in ten minutes?' This puts you back in the driving seat and gives you time to prepare.

7. Standing up when you take or make a call increases concentration and authority. Clenching your fist two or three times and then letting go builds up assertiveness. On the phone, your voice is the only part of you that 'shows'.

8. Distinguish between passive listening and active listening. *Active* listening is directed towards understanding what the other person means, purposeful in its aim to make the conversation succeed.

9. Give people time to explain why they've phoned you, while you wait your turn without interrupting. This gives *you* time to think out how to respond, and even to make some notes.

10. Experiment with choosing the *right* or *left* ear to listen with: this can put you more directly in touch with the side of the brain that provides the function you need most. Use the *right* ear when you are dealing with complex information, estimates or investments. Use the *left* ear when you want to come up with a brilliant idea or be more intuitive or sympathetic.

11. The expression on your face matters, even though the other person can't see you, because it can change your mood and your *voice* may pass that on. *Smiling* releases energy, standing up and smiling, even more energy.

12. Try out *method acting* on the telephone. Experiment with gestures, such as offering the palm of your hand, which puts

sympathy into your voice; or put determination into it by clenching your fist.

13. When a customer or a client phones, never make it difficult for them. Remember the MIETSY approach: *make it easy to say yes*.

14. Don't lie about why you're phoning. You'll be found out as soon as you give the real reason! It's usually better to come out in the open right from the start.

15. Write down straightaway one specific opportunity you expect to come up tomorrow, when you can use a new technique, a new piece of knowledge, a new understanding you have read about in this chapter.

10 The Fax Phenomenon

How to use faxes to negotiate, persuade and sell
How to follow up a letter or a phone call with a fax, so it doubles your
   chance of success
How to use a fax to set up a meeting and stack the cards on your side
How to build goodwill with a fax, especially in a good news situation
How to use a fax so it swings a decision your way

You may be surprised to hear that the first recorded use of the word 'fax' goes back well over forty years to 1948, when *Time* **magazine used it for 'facsimile' in the early days of photocopying machines.** But it was in the last years of the 1980s that 'fax' shot into everyday use everywhere in the world, as plug-in-and-go technology revolutionised intercity and international communications, using ordinary telephone lines to send and receive copies of letters, documents and graphics.

Fax, or *facsimile telegraphy* as it was called, is even older than the telephone and the first patented version is dated 1842! A Scotsman, Alexander Bain, invented a rudimentary system using two pendulums, one for transmitting and the other for receiving. The transmitter scanned metal letters and passed electrical pulses by wire to the receiving pendulum, causing it to oscillate over recording paper and leave legible smudges corresponding to the original letters.

High-speed facsimile transmission arrived by the 1960s, when complete issues of newspapers were transmitted to satellite branches for direct printing. *Postfax* came in 1974:

using the telephone network, it offered a fast way of sending documents between the main post offices of ten major cities. You took the document to the post office, filled in a form, and a facsimile, they said, would 'normally be in the hands of the recipient within three hours'. It sounds like winding up a 'gramophone' by hand!

Fax machines are now everyday high-tech, as commonplace and simple to use as the phone. The latest machines reduce transmission time to less than ten seconds for an A4 sheet of closely packed copy. As *payphone fax* services develop, we shall go up to machines in hotels, stations and airports, slip in a credit card and fax a letter or any other document to anywhere in the world. With a portable fax machine, linked to an acoustic coupler, executives can send their London or New York office specifications, letters, orders or sketches outlining customers' requirements, from a café table in Paris, a conference table in Hong Kong, or from anywhere where they can connect up to an ordinary telephone.

Fax is the quick way through the language barrier. You can fax a letter or document to a central service, such as British Telecom's International Division, where it is translated and faxed on to its destination. No time is lost. Fax has overcome the timezones altogether: transmissions can be programmed to time faxes to fit in with business hours in other countries. Colour fax for graphics has arrived and will soon become less expensive and more readily available.

All this is high-tech, and there is much more to come. How we *use* it depends as always on imagination and enterprise. Fax is infinitely adaptable and it is up to us to beat the competition by finding lively, innovative and creative applications. Even before the 1980s were left behind, Stuart Scher introduced *fax food* – he prints menu-cum-order-forms on perforated pages that slip into his customers' personal organisers. They fill in their orders and fax them to Choices, his City of London sandwich bar. Their packed lunches are then delivered on time and they avoid the lunch-hour queues!

Fax art was unveiled on 10 November 1989 when David Hockney faxed 144 sections of a giant painting from his studio in Los Angeles to a gallery near Bradford, to be assembled on the spot into a collage over 4m by 3m (14ft by 10ft), all ready for a fax art Private View.

One successful barrister has left his chambers in one of London's Inns of Court to bask all the year round in the sunshine of Florida. Solicitors say they get advice and opinions from him faster by fax from his deckchair on the sands of his private beach than they did by post, when much of his day in London was spent in traffic jams on the way to meetings. Faxing from a beach in Florida is for the highly privileged, but futurologists are predicting that the increasing use of fax will eventually lead to half the workforces of industrialised countries working from home, which may include deckchairs in back gardens or on balconies!

The fax timescale will go on shrinking until it becomes a mere flash; nothing is faster than fax for sending copy or illustrations. When codes and numbers are programmed, a *one-touch* key will send a fax to the right destination, or even to a number of destinations at the same time. If a line is engaged, it will automatically go on trying it. And nothing is more reliable, since fax machines give immediate confirmation that transmission has been effected and automatic line error correction makes sure everything you transmit is received.

Faxes are almost infallible and press-button high-tech has handed near-instant communication to us on a plate. What *we* do with it depends on our communication skills. At one level, a fax is a straightforward transmission of information: solicitors fax drafts of leases and contracts, engineers fax blueprints, surveyors fax estimates. At another level, a fax can help us to negotiate, persuade and sell: high-tech will carry the message but *we* have to use presentation and words that deliver the result we want. As always, the human factor is so often the deciding factor.

Because of its immediacy, fax has a person-to-person impact, almost as direct as talking to someone. We can make the most of this, when it's a short message, by writing a fax *by hand*. The person receiving it, even on the other side of the world, reads what we've written within minutes and the contact is close and personal. A handwritten fax is a spontaneous way of passing on thanks or encouragement. As you're writing it, *picture* the person reading it and you'll be more likely to strike the right note. Use a thick felt pen to add to the here-and-now, as well as to make the message come through bold and clear.

I am slowly losing my hearing and I was first attracted
to the fax when I realised it was a telephone for the
deaf . . . It's an aspect of high technology that's bringing
back intimacy – messages are handwritten again.

David Hockney

Fax works at its best as a hotline written contact between
one person and another, particularly when it's a *good news*
situation: it's like patting someone on the back or shaking their
hand – at a distance. When a supplier has made a real effort
to deliver ahead of time something you desperately need, or a
new customer has sent you a good order, an appreciative fax,
written by hand, is one of the best ways of saying 'Thank you',
catching the moment while you're still glowing with gratitude!

But be on guard against using a fax to break bad news. In
a *bad news* situation, there is always the temptation to avoid
a personal confrontation. That's not the way. If you've got to
inform someone that whether you like it or not, you are going
to let them down, you're much more likely to keep them on
your side by *speaking* to them. A bad news fax can be frustrating
– when something goes wrong, people want to ask questions,
react and be seen or heard to react. You stand a better chance
of smoothing over the problem if you put your fax pad on one
side and pick up the telephone. That will give the other person
the chance to let off steam and when they've finished, you can
do your best to make them feel better by saying how sorry you
are and how much you are doing to put things right.

Once that's all over, a fax is a useful follow-up, to confirm
what you've promised, to reassure and to underline that you
are doing everything that's possible. They will receive it a few
minutes after you have finished speaking to them and if you
write it out by hand, it keeps up the person-to-person contact
of your phone call.

On page 58 of this book, a television programme executive
explains how he uses a *teaser-fax*. Before setting off for a meeting
– which for him could be almost anywhere in the world – he
sends a fax to everyone he's planning to see, outlining what he's
going to tell them. He drafts it in a way that arouses expectancy

and interest but always hints there's something more to come, the 'just-wait-until-you-hear-about-this!' approach. A fax is the perfect way to set up a meeting: it can be right up-to-date and timed to arrive when *you* want it to.

If you want to use the *afterthought technique*, a fax makes an effective follow-up. You send a letter or make a phone call in the usual way, but keep back something new or dramatic. Wait a day or two (or an hour or two if it's after a phone call) and then send a *follow-up fax*, giving a new example of success or a new recommendation, or bringing out a spectacular plus factor you had 'overlooked'. A follow-up fax can help you clinch a deal by allowing you 'a second bite at the cherry'!

Is fax going to spell the end of letters? Perhaps even *paper* will become less necessary as texts on wordprocessor VDUs are faxed direct to micro-computers, to be read straight off-screen. In the 1920s, it was said the cinema was going to be the end of books; in the 1950s television was going to be the end of books; in the 1980s video-recorders were going to be the end of books. But it hasn't turned out that way, and the printed word on paper remains one of the most durable products of all time.

'Fax' is short for 'facsimile', a photocopy, suggesting a lack of substance and prestige. A letter has the status and authority of an original. At present faxes fade and have to be photocopied if a permanent record is required. Their legal status is uncertain. These problems will be overcome in time, just as fax haziness will give way to sharp definition. There is already an option on some expensive machines to take fax transmissions on ordinary paper which does not fade.

There remains a uniformity of presentation: faxes come out on the same kind of paper. Fax colour, when it becomes generally available, will allow for more individuality, but there will still be a certain *sameness*. This is where letters will find a new place, where there is less urgency and more need to make a strong individual impression.

Faxes account for over 20% of all business communications between the UK and the USA, and half the transmissions on telephone lines between the UK and Japan are fax messages. As fax becomes the main way to communicate in writing to sell goods, ideas and services, we shall have to work much harder to get results, to overcome the 'sameness' effect. The first step is not to take faxes for granted as marvellously convenient instant communication. The ready-to-hand facility of faxing, which is its great advantage, is also a danger, as it encourages us to send something off on the spur of the moment without working on it.

David Ogilvy, the Scotsman who was the first outsider to break in successfully on the New York advertising scene, knows more about communication than most people. 'Never send a letter or a memo on the day you write it,' he says, 'Read it aloud the next morning – and then edit it.' We are not likely to do that with a fax, because a fax, we believe, is something to be dashed off. Yet it could swing a decision one way or the other, make or break a sale, win or lose a contract – let that flash a warning light at you. This is the moment to think and reconsider, to work on your fax, even if it's handwritten, with the same attention you would give to a vital letter.

Not many people understand how important this is, so if you take the principle on board, it will keep you ahead of the crowd. Of course there's no reason why your carefully worked-on fax shouldn't *look* spontaneous – that, as David Ogilvy might say, is the art of *faxing clever*!

REVIEW OF COMMUNICATION SKILLS

1. Press-button high-tech has handed near-instant communication to us on a plate. What *we* do with it depends upon our communication skills.

2. Use a *handwritten* fax to pass on thanks or encouragement. As you're writing it, *picture* the person reading it and you'll be more likely to strike the right note. A thick felt pen adds to the immediacy, as well as making your message bold and clear.

3. A fax is the perfect hotline written contact in a *good news* situation. Because it's personal and spontaneous, use it like patting someone on the back or shaking their hand – at a distance.

4. Avoid sending a fax in a *bad news* situation. A 'bad news' fax is frustrating: when something goes wrong, people want to ask questions and let off steam. If you give them that chance you are much more likely to keep them on your side. Put your fax pad on one side and pick up the phone.

5. Use a *teaser-fax* to set up a meeting. Time it to arrive

an hour or so before you do. Outline what you're going to say and suggest you've got something up your sleeve – the 'just-wait-until-you-hear-about-this!' approach.

6. Use a fax for the *afterthought technique*. Send your letter or make a phone call in the usual way but keep something back. Wait a day or two (or an hour or two, if it's after a phone call) and send a *follow-up fax* bringing out something remarkable you had 'overlooked'.

7. Do not be misled into thinking a fax is *always* something to be dashed off. When a sale, a contract or a decision is in the balance, work on a fax just as hard and as long as you would on a vital letter, even though, when you send it, it may *look* casual. That's the art of *faxing clever*!

8. Write down straightaway one specific opportunity you expect to come up tomorrow when you can use a new technique, a new piece of knowledge, a new understanding you have read about in this chapter.

11 The Creative Pause

How to learn the power skills of successful negotiators
How to know what is going on in someone's mind
How to use the creative pause to get answers to questions
How to interview and be interviewed successfully
*How to use space in letters, reports, advertisements or brochures to achieve
 maximum impact*

**Jacques Séguéla is one of the most dynamic advertising
men in Paris and was chosen by François Mitterrand to
advise on publicity during the presidential campaign.**
Jacques is a professional communicator of the highest order,
who spends much of his working life selling ideas to other
people. He passes on to us one of the most valuable power
skills in communication:

> The most successful way to talk to people is to encourage
> them to talk to you.

This is the secret of top negotiators and in this chapter you will
find out how to use it. As you say less, you create a space which
the other person will fill and this presents you with a picture
of what is going on in their minds, gives you breathing-space
to marshal your own thoughts and puts you more in control
of the situation.
    Claude Lévi-Strauss, another Frenchman, worked in a very
different field from Jacques Séguéla. He was a professor at the
Sorbonne. Although he is famous for his lectures and books; he

concludes, 'Amongst us, language is used in a rather reckless way – we talk all the time, we ask questions about many things'. He believed that too many words, whether we are saying them or writing them, cause traffic jams in communication: they can actually stop our meaning getting through.

Most of us most of the time are stuck with using *words*. Here am I, using them at this moment, because that's what you expect in this situation. What would you do if you turned over and found the next half-a-dozen pages blank? You would think something has gone wrong and would take the book back to the bookshop. Yet think back . . . have you never experienced moments of near-perfect communication with someone, when words would only get in the way? 'For Godsake hold your tongue, and let me love!' pleaded John Donne. If you have never encountered that kind of communication, communication without words, it's worth opening yourself to the experience. Although words can do so much for us, it's an invaluable skill to learn when *not* to use them at work and in relationships.

The success of Terry Wogan on chat shows is because he is, according to the writer Simon Hoggart, 'probably the best exponent of the *creative pause* in broadcasting'. He establishes his authority by slowing down the action, leaving others to talk on, while he keeps silent.

It turned out that words don't always seem to have the high worth that we attribute to them. You can express a lot in the way people look at each other without having to go into a lengthy explanation.

Maeve Binchy,
watching the transformation of her
bestselling novel *Echoes* into a TV series.

Why do we say too much or write too much? Almost invariably because we are over-anxious. When something is important to us, getting a job done, making something happen, convincing someone or helping someone in trouble, it's human nature to be afraid of failing. So we try too hard. We have all had the experience of being exposed to someone talking too much. The result is oversell and we turn away. But when you hold back and take Jacques Séguéla's advice to let the other person do more of the talking, while you remain still, you will see remarkable things happen.

Thomas Hardy said of someone, 'That man's silence is wonderful to listen to'. Some of the most charismatic people have achieved their effect by silence. Michael Foster, who taught philosophy at Christ Church, Oxford, is said to have had the precious and exceptional quality of inspiring courage and understanding by saying so little. One of his students remembered his silences as 'nutritious because he did not pretend to know the right answers'. It takes great restraint to leave a question hovering in mid-air instead of rushing in with an instant comment. For important questions there is often no cut-and-dried answer and if you come up with a quick off-the-cuff solution, the question is dismissed too soon. A *creative pause* enables us to stay in front of a question long enough for a synthesis to emerge. Sometimes the best answer to 'Well, what do you think?' is 'I'm still thinking!'

John Gielgud, a great actor, believes *pauses are as important as speech* and he rehearses silence with the same care as he rehearses dialogue. Not only can we plan pauses in advance in the theatre, we can plan them in real-life situations and can anticipate when to stop and allow space for the other person to come in. The creative pause is taught on management courses by acting out situations that occur regularly in our work. Here are two scenarios, with pauses 'written into' the script.

Suppose you have gathered a handful of people together to discuss a problem or something that has gone wrong or to decide on a plan. You explain what the meeting is about and wait for someone to make a contribution. No-one says anything for a minute or two, so you come up with your explanation or with a suggested solution – effectively killing off any ideas that might be sprouting in someone else's mind.

Good theatre directors use rehearsals to create a climate in which actors are free to bring their own ideas to the play, as directors are well aware that unless they hold back they might miss out on valuable creative contributions. Similarly at a meeting, once you have outlined the problem, you can say, 'That's the problem. Let's take a few minutes out to think what **we can do about it'. During those few minutes, you hold back** from saying anything more: the silence will produce a certain tension, which is one of the great values of a creative pause.

Another situation is when you give people something to look at, a draft of a letter, or a report, or a sketch for a design or an estimate and while they're looking at it you explain and justify what you have done. The effect is to divide their attention – they have to try to listen to you and at the same time look at what you've put in front of them. It is better to sit there quietly and wait while they look at what you have given them. Even when they look up, there is no need to say anything: leave space for them to come in with their comments and reserve your energy to deal with any doubts that may arise. Radio and television can give us the wrong idea – both demand a rapid fire of questions and answers because they're always operating against the clock. That's show business, which is not at all the same as real life.

When we know a lot about something, there's a tendency to go on talking for too long. It takes skill and practice to know when it is valuable to help someone follow an argument, or when you are spelling everything out too laboriously. A useful exercise is to listen to yourself talking to children, because that's when we so often over-simplify and talk down. If they begin to look bored, let that be a warning and remember the same thing can happen when you are talking to anyone.

The more clearly we remember our own childhood . . . the more we can help. I can remember those few grown-ups who did not talk down to me and the many who did and were therefore bores or made fools of themselves.
> Dr Dermod MacCarthy,
> *Communication Between Children and Doctors*

A research group studying the skills of successful negotiators discovered that whereas most people reveal their anxiety to reach an agreement by presenting too many arguments, out-standing negotiators say less than half as much within the same period of time. They use *fewer* reasons to sell the case they are putting forward, a technique which gives greater assurance to the other side, as well as focussing on the strongest arguments, leaving out others that might more easily be countered.

The law of diminishing returns operates in negotiations: there is an optimum point where our words produce the maximum result and when we go beyond that, the more words we use, the more likely we are to achieve a lesser result. In a discussion of any kind, there is usually a peak – marked sometimes when the other person begins to talk as if your proposition is their idea – and that's the moment to use the creative pause. Look out for this *top dead centre*, the point of maximum response, and when you recognise it, hold back and let the other party convince themselves. This is the hallmark of the most brilliant negotiators, who know that after a peak the next direction must be downwards.

The research group also found top negotiators spend *twice* as much time during a meeting *asking questions*. Questions slow down a discussion and create more pauses. If you are going into a meeting of any kind, an interview for a job or an encounter with someone who might buy your product or service, plan and memorise in advance a number of questions that you can call upon. Use a question whenever you want to create a pause to give you more time to think.

A direct question can have an aggressive edge. If it's an interview for a job and you ask 'What are my prospects in, say, two years' time?' this may put the other person on the defensive, which won't do you any good. When you're going to ask something difficult, it's better to use a lead-in, such as 'Would you mind if I ask a question?' or 'There's something I'd be grateful if you could give me advice on'. This encourages people to be more expansive, more likely to meet you at least half-way.

When you are in the hot seat, and it's an interview for an appointment or with a potential customer, concentrate on *listening* rather than talking. When you are asked a question there is no need to rush in and answer it immediately. If you pause, your answer may carry more weight. Listen to how politicians start answering questions even before the question is formulated. They are committed to a fixed undeviating line and so often do not seem to be answering the real questions that are put to them. That is political rhetoric and will not work for us if we are truly seeking to convince someone. Instead, make sure the people you are talking to have really finished asking their questions. If you wait, they may express a question in another way, or even start answering it themselves!

When you are handling the interview – with an applicant for a job, a representative who wants to sell you something, a solicitor or anyone else from whom you want advice – the worst thing you can do is to talk too much yourself. You are there to find out, not to expound. If it's a solicitor or a consultant of any kind, remember you're paying them for *their* time and if you take up most of it by talking, you are wasting your money. There are varying recommendations about the proportion of talking time between an interviewer and the other person. Generally it's suggested that if interviewers talk more than 20% of the time, they are talking too much. It is not, of course, realistic to calculate these things precisely. It is sufficient to remember that *time* is a major factor in interviews, and you have to work at using the time available to find out what you want to know.

Most of us are usually short of time and time for real communication is too often given a low priority. If the person you are talking to senses you are in a hurry, they will feel on the run and your discussion will become tense and usually unproductive. It is a fact that when you say less yourself, so the other person does more of the talking, they will feel you are giving them much more time than you really are and will go away more satisfied with the meeting.

People who are half convinced will often do the rest of the work themselves, if you keep quiet and let them get on with it. An experienced executive in charge of a presentation team will often have a secret way of warning his group to stop talking. He may take off his glasses or scratch the side of his nose, or give whatever signal has been prearranged as a warning to keep quiet and let the other side have their say. The creative pause is so valuable that you should plan how you're going to use it just as carefully as you plan what you are going to say.

In print, the direct equivalent of the creative pause is

space.

An A4 sheet of paper for a letter that requires only three lines isn't always a waste of paper because the *space* around those three lines will focus the reader's attention on the one thing you are saying. It's different with leases or contracts or other legal documents that people have to sign. Then they are prepared to work their way through each line, no matter how closely packed it may be.

In other cases, reading and recall tests demonstrate that a letter or brochure packed with copy will at best be half-read, half-skimmed, so only about half the words are read. For all we know, many people will read the half that's *less* important to us! Take the same letter or brochure, cut the words to half or preferably fewer still, surround what is left with *space*, and readership and recall leap up.

The Green Party demonstrated how effective space can be, even in a small advertisement. A coupon at the bottom invited people to apply for membership of the party. Above there was an empty space, except for seven words in the middle. They were printed very small, but because of the white space around them, the eye was irresistibly drawn to what they said:

At last
there's a glimmer
of hope

A whole-page advertisement in a national newspaper is expensive. Volkswagen took a series of pages measuring 580mm (about 23in) from top to bottom. 480mm (about 19in) were filled with empty grey space. In what little space was left at the bottom they told us:

In our view, you're looking at the
closest rival to the *Golf GTi*.

That empty grey space cost a lot of money but in the newspapers where the advertisement appeared, more people looked at and *read* the message than any of the other advertisements. Empty space, well used, can be a marvellous investment!

The Hanson financial group took whole pages in newspapers to announce their annual profits and dividends to shareholders. There was no long-winded company report. Right at the top was the brief statement

25 YEARS OF HANSON
SUMMED UP IN ONE LINE

The rest of the page was empty, except for a thin wavy line of tiny letters going up from bottom left to top right. As you peered closer, you read 'For the 25th consecutive year, Hanson announces record profit, dividends and earnings per share. . .' The line curved its way upwards across the empty space, giving a few details. Expensive *empty* space made the point for Hanson because most people who opened the newspapers that day read that thin line of words. And they remembered it was going *upwards*!

In the hardest, toughest negotiations, the skill of saying less or writing less can win the day. We are so surrounded by noise, verbiage, instant comment, that we seriously devalue economy in the use of words: using fewer words is a marvellous option – and it's always available to you.

REVIEW OF COMMUNICATION SKILLS

1. 'The most successful way to talk to people is to encourage them to talk to you'. When you say less, you create a space for the other person to fill. How they fill it presents you with a picture of what is going on in their mind, gives you breathing-space to marshal your thoughts, and puts you more in control of the situation.

2. When you are too quick with an off-the-cuff answer to some questions, you miss an opportunity. A *creative pause* enables you to stay in front of a question long enough for a synthesis to emerge.

3. For interviews and meetings, plan pauses *in advance*, so

you know when to stop and allow time for the other person to come in.

4. At a meeting you've called to find a solution to a situation, outline the problem but don't go any further. Instead say something like 'Let's take a few minutes to think what we can do about this'. During those few minutes, hold back to make others come forward with *their* ideas.

5. When you give people something to look at – the draft of a letter or a report, a sketch, an estimate – *keep quiet and still* while they're looking at it. Even when they look up, there's no need to say anything right away. Reserve your energy to deal with any doubts that present themselves.

6. If you're an expert on something, be on guard against over-explaining and talking down to people. If they begin to look bored, that's a warning to say less.

7. Research shows that within the same period of time top negotiators say less than half as much as run-of-the-mill salesmen. They use fewer reasons to convince other people and spend *twice* as much time asking questions.

8. Be on the lookout in a negotiation for a peak, marked sometimes when the other side starts to convince themselves. That's the moment to let the *creative pause* work for you. Oversell makes people walk away.

9. When you are interviewing people to find out something, make sure they do at least 75% of the talking. If you're paying for their time and take up most of it by talking yourself, you're wasting your money!

10. It's a fact that when you say less and let the other person do more of the talking, they will feel you are giving them much more time than you really are and will go away more satisfied with the meeting.

11. When people ask questions, it's all right to pause before answering. You may find they will then express the question in another way, which will help you, or even start answering it themselves.

12. Readership and recall tests demonstrate a letter or brochure

packed with copy will at best be half-read, half-skimmed, and that many people will read the bits that are *less* important to you. When you want to rivet your reader's attention on what really matters, all you have to do is surround it by. . .

space.

13. Write down straightaway one specific opportunity you expect to come up tomorrow when you can use a new technique, a new piece of knowledge, a new understanding you have read about in this chapter.

12 Active Listening

How active listening brings authority and leadership
How to direct successful new starts on new ideas
How to convert passive listening to active listening
How to transfer important information into your long-term memory
How to use a secret technique to focus your attention, no matter what
distractions get in the way

A world study of leading achievers in all fields, from industry to universities, presents us with a vital key to success: most people who reach the top spend very much more of their time *listening* than the people who don't make it. It seems that success in our work, and in our personal lives as well, has a great deal to do with skill at listening to other people.

If we are good technicians, able to do the job well ourselves, that's valuable of course. But if it stops there, we are not likely to rise above the rank and file. To move up the ladder, we have to develop authority and leadership, which relate to our ability to get others to do their jobs better, so we make the most effective use of human resources around us. The first step is to learn what management courses call *active listening*. Whether it's your own business employing half-a-dozen people, or whether you work in a multinational with a staff of thousands, listening is one of the most critical of all management skills.

Marketing in its widest sense is the basis of success in every buying-and-selling activity, which includes selling ourselves in whatever area we work. As we approach the 21st century, key marketing factors are changing at an ever-increasing pace;

the prescription – not just for success but for survival – is innovation, making more starts on new ideas. If these are at random, it's like playing roulette. The only way to direct them is through responsiveness to the marketplace: we must learn to listen to customers and potential customers, to employers and potential employers.

John Donne, the 17th-century metaphysical poet whose passionate plea for silence illumined the last chapter, provides this chapter with a warning, as urgent now as when it was written over 350 years ago:

> No man is an Island, entire of itself;
> every man is a piece of the continent,
> a part of the main.

Listening is the skill that connects us. The Sperry Corporation goes on record as stating that research shows them good listening is one of their greatest strengths in the marketplace, and 'is fundamental to the way we do business'.

But what's all the fuss about? Don't we already listen most of the time? Rabbi Lionel Blue answers that question with a present-day parable, set in a psychiatric hospital. A young psychotherapist, just beginning his clinical career, has spent the whole day listening to disturbed patients. By early evening, he is shattered and goes into the consultants' restaurant to order a double brandy. An experienced colleague is there, happily relaxing over a pre-dinner drink. The young man confronts him:

'How can you listen to all these terrible problems and keep your calm?' The older man shrugs.

'Who's listening?' he asks.

The senior consultant knows there is a world of difference between *hearing* and *listening*. Hearing is automatic: our eardrums are so highly-tuned that a sound vibration has only to disturb the surface of them by a 100-millionth of a millimetre and it is picked up. *Listening* depends on how we connect and respond when vibrations set up in the inner ear send their messages to the brain through the auditory nerve. Animals visibly prick up their ears when they focus their nervous systems on sounds. We cannot do that, but we *can* jolt our minds into more intense concentration and convert 'hearing' to *listening*.

In the Phone Power chapter we separated passive from active

listening. *Passive listening* is like listening to background music: we are half aware of the melody, we may unconsciously walk in time to the rhythm, but our attention to it is minimal. *Active listening* is interpreting what we hear, working at understanding what it means and making a deliberate evaluation that helps us decide what to *do* about it.

Tests show repeatedly how incompetent most people are at listening: after listening to someone for ten minutes, an hour later untrained listeners usually retain only half of what was said. By the next morning, only a quarter is remembered. What a waste! It is demonstrated on courses that when we learn the listening skills in this chapter, our recall can be trebled at the very least – think what that would mean in your work, where listening is often the most important source of information. *Active listening* presents you with a map of what you're dealing with and when you have a map in front of you, it's so much easier to go in the right direction!

We are involved in a number of different listening situations. There is the one-to-one situation, an exchange between you and one other person. Or it can be a discussion in a small group, up to a dozen or so people. Or you may be part of an audience of 30 or 300 or 3,000. Each situation requires an adaptation of listening skills, although they nearly always have one major problem in common: we have to live with the fact that the spoken word cannot be 'read' again. Although it might be possible sometimes to record what is being said, mostly when you are listening to someone that is the one and only chance to take it in. If you don't get it right first time round and really understand the message, you may miss out for ever on an important opportunity to develop your career or your business, or to enhance the quality of an important relationship.

Active listening starts with being aware of the blocks that get in the way, that filter out so much of what is being said to us. These are the ones that affect us most:

1. Our personal reaction towards the speaker – their appearance, mannerisms, accent – distracts our attention. We must learn to set aside any personal bias, or it will obscure what is being said. The next time you are listening to someone who arouses strong personal reactions, make a point of deliberately keeping the medium in the background and making only one thing count for you – the *message*.

2. When listening involves a group of people or you are part of a large audience, distractions can easily get in the way. A good-looking man, an attractive woman, outside noises may all nibble away at your attention so you miss whole sentences. We have to put on imaginary *blinkers* to keep our attention focussed on what is being said, deliberately excluding everything else.

3. When you are listening, any chance remark can send you off on irrelevant associations, and for a few seconds – or even minutes – you are 'miles away'. Boredom has the same effect and allows your attention to drift off. The most effective way to prevent this is to use, as a kind of *mantra*, the reason why you are there listening. *Mantra* is a Sanskrit word for a sacred formula used in meditation to focus the mind. Here are examples of how you can use this ancient teaching: if you are at a sales conference, your mantra could be *Sales Effectiveness*. The moment you feel your mind wandering, you repeat those words to yourself and they will bring you back to what you are listening for. Suppose it's a management course and something reminds you of last year's holiday on a Greek island. As your mind drifts away to the sands and seas of the Aegean, bring it back by repeating to yourself *Better Management*.

Mantras have been used by Buddhist monks for over two thousand years to keep their minds centred. The same formula can be adapted just as effectively in the 1990s to increase listening skills.

4. Emotions can rapidly take over and prevent us listening effectively: perhaps what is being said makes you fearful, or you envy the style of the speaker, or something makes you angry. Whatever it may be, emotions are there all the time just below the surface, waiting to come up to cloud our judgement and block effective listening.

In the area of emotions the human species is in a class by itself. We don't just possess the emergency emotions of fear and rage. We have subtle small passions. We have pride, shame and guilt. We feel hurt and touched. These small emotions . . . commingle with our intelligence in guiding our actions.

Dr Willard Gaylin, *Rediscovering Love*

Emotions are the hardest of all blocks to deal with but the mantra technique can help us. If you are listening to a customer and emotions get in the way, you could use *Keep The Business* as your mantra to focus your attention.

5. The last block that comes between us and effective listening is the temptation to think ahead to what *you* are going to ask or say. You see and hear this going on all the time in discussions on television. By thinking ahead, maybe you will score a point with some brilliant comment. But you could pay a high price: you may miss out on something very important that is being said.

No two situations are alike, and only you can decide which has first priority at that moment: making an impression for yourself, or listening as effectively as you can to the other person. It's almost impossible to do both, so once you've made a value judgement, keep to it!

When the blocks are out of the way and you are listening with real attention, there are three essential principles:

1. *Interpretation*: Work at understanding what someone means. This goes beyond taking in the words they are saying, it's getting at the meaning behind the words. They may be telling you the situation cannot be changed, there is no more 'money on the table', or they may be suggesting there's room for negotiation. Listen *between the lines* for the real meaning.

2. *Evaluation*: Weigh up the *value* of what is being said. Is it something you can use, or is it in the end neither here nor there? It's almost like deciding whether to buy a new piece of equipment – you work out how you can use it and whether it's worth the cost. When you're listening, evaluate what something can do for *you*.

3. *Reaction*: What are you going to *do* about what you are listening to? Or will you do nothing? Just as a good report should always end on action to be taken, so *active listening* requires you to decide what to do next.

These three principles are backed up by day-to-day listening skills that are easy to learn. First comes *preparation*: before you go in to listen to someone, whether it's one person, a small group or a lecture, try to find time to go over relevant background material. This may mean quickly reading through a report, looking at correspondence or memos, looking at notes. Where such preparation is possible it provides an outline, so as you're listening, you can mentally slot what is being said into the right places.

Next is the skill known as *chunking*. As you listen to someone, separate what they are telling you into *chunks* of information, as it is much easier to take in organised pieces of information than to handle separate sentences. Chunking plays a big part in what psychologists call 'encoding', a technique which converts information into coherent shapes which are more readily stored in your memory. Whoever is talking to you may help by *slowing down* at certain points – unconsciously or otherwise – and this often indicates that those points are of particular importance. Look out for this.

Anything that is *said* passes quickly and our recall drops away fast – we have already seen how little the untrained listener retains by the next morning. There is a huge difference between *short-term* and *long-term* memory: all new information coming your way goes into your short-term memory and fades away quickly, unless you *consciously* transfer it to your long-term memory. There is only one way to do this, which is to go over the information again.

When someone is talking, there is no rewind button! But you can *make notes*, which you can use afterwards to move information from short-term to long-term memory. Never be afraid of making notes, even at a one-to-one meeting; the other person will usually take it as a compliment, because you are implying that what they are saying is important enough for you to write down.

Of course you can't write everything down: if you try to write too much it will confuse you and distract the other person. Speakers usually make points and then amplify them, adding examples and more detail: in note-taking, aim to put down the central points only. Shorthand systems using ordinary letters of the alphabet are much easier to learn than complicated systems of symbols. There is also an easy alternative that some consultants and journalists use. It takes less than an hour to learn and can easily double your note-taking speed. There are eleven simple abbreviations, all easy to remember, because they connect immediately with the words they represent:

r= *are*
s= *is* or *as*
t= *it*
u= *you*
v= *have*
y= *why*
2= *to*
/= *the*
+= *with, including* or *and*
−= *less* or *without*
:= *therefore, hence* or *so*

In addition to using these abbreviations, you leave out as many *vowels* as possible, so long as the word is still easy to recall, and improvise your own short-cuts. Here are two sentences, written out in this 'instant' shorthand, to show how it works:

This is an easy way of taking notes more quickly. With practice you can soon *double* your ordinary writing speed.

Ths s n esy wy f tkng nts mr kwkly. Wth prctc u cn sn *dbl* yr ordnry rtg spd.

The success of this marketing plan depends on making sure we have the right price structure. So it is important to talk to as many potential customers without delay.

/ scs f ths mrktg pln dpnds n mkg sr we v / rt prc strctr. : t s imprtnt 2 tk 2 s mny ptntl cstmrs – dly.

Practise this for five minutes a day, by copying out one of the paragraphs in this book. Within a week it will become part of you and you can expect before long to take notes at least twice as fast as before.

The value of notes is to go over them again as soon as possible after you have finished listening – you may be able to do this on the train home when you can use a pocket note-recorder to add more detail. This process transfers information from short-term to long-term memory. Of course you won't need to do this every time, but when you've been listening to something especially important, or something you have to write a report on, that's the time to work in this way. It's like putting something on mental file for future use, instead of throwing it away.

Asking questions is an essential part of active listening. The purpose of listening is to understand and if there is something you haven't understood, do *not* leave the room without finding out! People are often afraid to ask simple questions and go away without ever knowing. If you are like that, take advice and take heart from Tom Peters, one of the most successful consultants on the West Coast of America. He tells us 'Mostly, it's the *dumb* elementary questions, followed up by a dozen even more elementary questions, that yield the pay dirt!'

Asking questions is one thing: interrupting is something else. If you are taking part in a discussion, watch *your* input! If you say too much and interrupt all the time, not only will you alienate others, you will end up listening more to yourself, which will only tell you what you already know.

When it's a small group or a one-to-one encounter, it's important to *look* as if you are listening. Look at the person who is speaking and *react*: show surprise, nod with agreement, smile at the funny bits, look serious when necessary – anything to interact. This has a double effect: it helps *you* to concentrate, and it encourages the other person to tell you more. Margaret Thatcher, who does more talking than most of us, once said 'It's when they sit there like suet puddings I find it difficult!' If you make it difficult for the people talking to you, you will get less out of them.

Nothing has a better effect on the actors than the still-ness of the African audiences . . . the African is of course capable of enormous energy, but also of enormous still-ness, and this still, concentrated attention was the most precious thing to play to.

Peter Brook, *The Shifting Point*

We live in a world that becomes noisier every year and this builds up the habit of listening mechanically or even switching off altogether. If you transfer that habit to situations where real listening could save your job, keep a customer, or open up a great opportunity, you will lose out. When listening is important, think of your ears as flesh-and-blood ear-trumpets – which is exactly how they function – and this will make you focus more intently on what is being said. Practise being *all ears*! *Active listening* can make an incalculable difference to your work and also to personal relationships. Helen Gurley Brown, who developed the present-day *Cosmopolitan* magazine, tells us to stop what we're doing and *really listen* to our wives and husbands, 'to the dull stuff along with the good stuff. It will keep you out of the divorce court, and divorce lawyers from getting all your money'.

REVIEW OF COMMUNICATION SKILLS

1. People who reach the top spend very much more of their time *listening* than people who don't make it.

2. *Active listening* brings the authority and leadership to enable you to make the most of the human resources around you.

3. In the 1990s the prescription not just for success but also for survival, is innovation. The only way to *direct* new starts on new ideas is to listen to customers and potential customers, to employers and potential employers.

4. *Hearing* is automatic, as your eardrums pick up the slightest sound. *Listening* depends on how you connect and respond when vibrations set up in the inner ear send their messages to the brain.

5. Tests repeatedly show most people are incompetent at listening, even though listening is often our most important source of information. *Active listening* presents you with a map of what you are dealing with, and when you have a map in front of you, it's so much easier to go in the right direction!

6. Listening is usually a one-off opportunity and if you don't get it right, you may miss out for ever on an important opportunity to develop your career or your business, or to enhance the quality of an important relationship.

7. These are the blocks that get in the way of effective listening:

- Your personal reaction towards the speaker. Set aside personal bias: keep the medium in the background and focus on the *message*.
- Other people in the room or noises outside distract attention. Put on imaginary *blinkers* and focus your attention on what is being said.
- Irrelevant associations and boredom make your mind wander. Invent your own *mantra* to remind you what you are listening for.
- Emotions can take over, cloud your judgement and take up all your attention. This is the hardest block to deal with, but the mantra technique can help. Invent a mantra and use it to bring back your attention.
- At times it's an almost irresistible temptation to think ahead to what *you* are going to ask or say. Decide which has first priority: making an impression for yourself or listening as effectively as you can to the other person.

8. Work on the three essential principles of active listening:

(i) *Interpretation*: Listen 'between the lines' for the real meaning of what is being said.

(ii) *Evaluation*: Work out how you can *use* what you are listening to.

(iii) *Reaction*: Decide what to *do* with the new information coming your way.

9. Wherever possible, *prepare* for listening by reading relevant background material. Preparation provides an outline, so you mentally slot what is being said into the right places.

10. Use *chunking*. Separate what you're being told into *chunks* of information; this converts information into coherent shapes which are more readily stored in your memory.

11. When you're listening, remember there's no rewind button! So make *notes*, which you can use afterwards to transfer anything important from *short-term* memory to *long-term* memory. If you don't already know a shorthand system, it takes less than an hour to learn the 'instant' shorthand described in this chapter, which will double your note-taking speed.

12. *Asking questions* is an essential listening skill. Don't be afraid to ask even simple questions – anything is better than

leaving the room without finding out: you may never get another chance.

13. Watch *your* input! If you say too much and interrupt all the time, you will end up listening to yourself, which will only tell you what you know already.

14. Think of your ears as flesh-and-blood ear-trumpets, which will make you focus more intently on what is being said to you. Practise being *all ears*.

15. Write down straightaway one specific opportunity you expect to come up tomorrow when you can use a new technique, a new piece of knowledge, a new understanding you have read about in this chapter.

13 Can You Speak Their Language?

How to communicate in the multilingual marketplace
How to talk to people who have limited fluency in English
How to be sensitive to different attitudes and feelings in another country
How to handle situations abroad, when something goes wrong
How to use a handful of words in a foreign language to establish a rapport

The talk now is of the hypermarketplace, multinational, multiracial and multilingual. Theodore Levitt, head of marketing studies at Harvard Business School, is a prophet of globalisation and he advises companies to 'learn to operate as if the world were one large market, ignoring superficial regional and national differences'.

This message is echoed by the Institut Européan d'Administration des Affaires – *Insead* for short – at Fontainebleau, just outside Paris, an institute which *Fortune*, leading US business magazine, calls 'the Rolls-Royce of European business schools'. *Insead* works on the basis that management in the 1990s and beyond will consist of teams that effectively combine different national characteristics.

In Europe, internationalism started with the Treaty of Rome which established the European Community in 1957. Britain joined in 1973 and there are now eleven other member countries: Belgium, Denmark, France, Germany, Greece, Ireland, Italy, Luxembourg, the Netherlands, Portugal and Spain. At midnight on 31 December 1992, the remaining barriers come down to open up a single market of more than 320m Euro-consumers, a third larger than the vast American market and more than twice the size of the market in Japan.

But there is this big difference: the European market will be *multilingual*, speaking *ten* different languages. Add to that the many other languages spoken in the world hypermarket and we have the makings of a new Tower of Babel. How will you cope, as you move from a meeting with a supplier in Germany to a customer in Paris to an important new contact in Tokyo? This is perhaps even more urgent for the British and Americans, two of the most linguistically xenophobic of nations. At least 90% of US executives working in Japan do not bother to learn Japanese; and the British are warned of the shortage of language skills by the Department of Trade and Industry, which adds 'there is clear evidence of a direct link between export performance and proficiency in foreign languages'. The situation becomes more pressing as 6,000 men dig a clearway under the English Channel!

Even the smallest of companies, not even involved in export, are caught up in this linguistic situation, as they will find themselves on their home ground dealing with so many more foreign people coming to the UK on business. In a four-year period, the number of Japanese companies setting up in Britain has quadrupled. It's a dilemma. On the one hand, according to Jo Baxter of British Telecom's International Division, 'Talking to someone in their own language is a courtesy you can't put a price on. It proves you mean business'. On the other hand, there are so many languages required to meet the challenge of globalisation.

The fact that you can read this book gives you a huge linguistic head start. If you were born in the United States, Great Britain, Australia, New Zealand, Canada, South Africa or any other country where the English language is your birthright, you already speak the most international language in the world.

In Eastern Europe, political revolution has been followed by a linguistic revolution. As Russian ceased to be a compulsory second language, English took over, and Poland, Czechoslovakia, Hungary and the other Eastern European countries are clamouring for more and more teachers of English. In the Netherlands, an education minister even suggested Dutch universities should use English as the main language of teaching. It caused an uproar but shows which way the linguistic wind is blowing.

If there is one safe prediction for the 1990s, it is that the English language will become universally recognised as the most important key to economic development and personal betterment.

Richard Francis,
director-general, British Council

English is the official language of the Olympic Games, wherever they are held, the language of international scientific and economic conferences, of flying and shipping, and the obligatory second language – or at least a smattering of it – for every waiter, taxi-driver, hotel receptionist and air hostess.

Randolph Quirk, president of the British Academy, tells us *'more than half* of the people who use English in the world have not learned it as their first language'. We shall all find ourselves increasingly talking English to people who know it only as a second language and there are valuable skills you can learn, which you can apply when talking to people whose knowledge of English is not as assured as your own. It's not just a matter of speaking more slowly or louder; in fact, it's worth noting that when you speak too loud, your diction is not as clear and it's more difficult for someone to understand you. One chief executive in New York has been known to complain, at heated meetings, 'Not so loud please. I can't hear you!'

Tests have demonstrated there are two useful communication skills when you are speaking to people who have to work at understanding English: *chunking* – grouping information into coherent, easily manageable bits, and breaking up the content of what you are saying into clausal units of no more than *seven* words. Dr David Weeks, neuropsychologist at the Royal Edinburgh Hospital, has established that seven objects or seven chunks of data is the number the average person can handle without stress. As stress is an enemy to good communication, you should aim to keep within that limit. With practice, you can use these techniques in a relaxed way so it sounds like normal discourse.

When you are talking to a group of people in another country, it is not always easy to know how competent each one of them is in the use of English, which makes it more important than ever to arrange what you have to say into *chunks*. Pausing between each chunk has a much better result than talking slowly, which can easily seem patronising. In this situation you have to watch faces intently, looking for signs that something may not be properly understood. People don't usually like being asked, 'Have you understood that?' as it puts them in an inferior position. It's better to ask a question such as 'Would you like me to go over that again?'

Even when people know a second language well, they instinctively revert to their own language for numeration. When you go into Italian food shops, for example, in English-speaking countries, you hear the owners speaking good English, but as it comes to adding up the bill, you hear them counting in *Italian*. Remember that when you are going through costs with people in another country: no matter how good their English may be, go over *figures* extra carefully and if possible set them up on display, so they can be *seen* as figures.

Of course, many people in other countries are almost bilingual and you can talk to them in English as readily as you can to people in London or New York. But even then it's important to be sensitive to differences of attitudes and feelings. John Harvey-Jones, former chairman of ICI, feels the growing use of English as the language of international business is a trap and 'the mere fact that one stays in the same sort of hotel almost anywhere in the world, that one drives the same sort of car . . . gives a superficial feeling of sameness, which is desperately misleading'. Some export executives make a point of staying in local hotels rather than big international ones, and eating in small local cafés rather than tourist restaurants. Such things are a matter of personal choice but getting a *feeling* for another country and the people who live in it is a valuable help in communicating with them successfully, even if they do speak English fluently.

When something goes wrong, people are under more stress and are usually more at ease speaking their own language, unless they are truly bilingual. Earlier in this book, it was reported that a study revealed it costs five times more to go out and get a new customer than to keep one you already have: if it's a customer in another country, you can double that cost. So when something has gone wrong, that's the time to communicate with people in their own language. Although you may be in the habit of writing to them in English, this is the moment to use a good translation agency. If you are speaking to them in person or on the telephone, speak *their* language, if you can. If you can't, use an interpreter. These are positive ways of showing your concern to put something right.

If you ever have to work through an interpreter, there are a few skills to learn. Have them stand or sit either beside or on one side, slightly in front of you. Never position them behind you. Actors call this being *upstaged*: if the interpreter is just behind you, people you are talking to tend to look past you, at them even when *you* are speaking. When the interpreter is talking, look at the other people as if you are speaking yourself. As the interpreter finishes a particular section, come in as positively as you can with the next thing you want to say, to demonstrate *you* are clearly in charge.

Videoconferences will become commonplace in a few years, covering the whole world. As British Telecom claims, it will no longer be 'one of those ultra-expensive, super-executive gimmicks that big firms employ to massage executive egos'. Small businesses will use this as an economic, time-saving way of setting up face-to-face meetings with customers and suppliers in other countries, simply by booking an hour at a videoconference centre.

If you are involved in a videoconference, using English to people less at home with the language, be extra careful with your pacing. Put even longer pauses between chunks, and work at the seven-words-to-a-sentence principle. A videoconference may be 'like being in the same room', but misunderstandings occur more easily because the strength of person-to-person contact is diluted. A misunderstanding always undermines confidence. If in doubt, use an interpreter, who can work simply as a *voice over*: people at the receiving end just hear the interpreter, while they stay looking at you on the monitor.

Executives, international troubleshooters and special envoys know the value of learning even a handful of words of the language of a country they are visiting. The people you are dealing with may speak perfect English but it's a courtesy which establishes another kind of rapport if you can say, in their own language, a few expressions such as 'Good morning' or 'Good afternoon', 'Hello', 'Goodbye'. If you can take it further and learn to say, 'Thank you for letting me come to talk to you' or something like that, that's a warm opening to a meeting, even if afterwards you continue by speaking in English.

Experience shows that a private lesson of an hour or two with a native speaker of the language is an investment that always pays off. You will feel more confident yourself, and the people you are talking to will respect the effort you've made. Whatever the language, no matter how obscure or difficult, be sure to learn, practise and *use* at least the words for 'Thank you' and 'Cheers!'

REVIEW OF COMMUNICATION SKILLS

1. When someone has limited fluency in English, avoid speaking too slowly, as if you're talking to an idiot. They won't like it, any more than you would. And don't speak extra loudly as that will distort your diction. Their knowledge of English may be limited but that doesn't make them either stupid or deaf!

2. Use *chunking* when talking to people who have to work at understanding English. Group information into easily manageable bits and pause a little longer than usual after each section.

3. Break up what you are saying into clausal units of about seven words. That may seem short but it has been shown it makes listening much less tiring for people who do not speak English fluently.

4. People prefer not to be asked 'Have you understood that?' as it can put them in an inferior position. Instead ask a question such as 'Would you like me to go over that again?'

5. Be particularly careful when you're talking about *figures*, as even people who know English well often revert to their own language for numeration. When possible, set figures up on display so people can see them as figures as well as hear them as words.

6. Language apart, it's a valuable help in communicating successfully abroad if you are sensitive to differences of attitudes

and feelings. You will learn more if you venture away from the standard tourist circuit.

7. People are under more stress when something goes wrong and at such times want to speak or read their own language, unless they are truly bilingual. You will often find it easier to save the situation or keep a customer by using a translator or an interpreter – unless, of course, you are fluent in the other language.

8. No matter how obscure or difficult the language of a country you are visiting, learn, practise and *use* words for a few phrases such as 'Good morning', 'Good afternoon', 'Hello', 'Goodbye', 'Thank you' . . . and 'Cheers!'

9. Before your next journey to meet contacts in a foreign country, write down one specific opportunity you expect to come up when you can use a new technique, a new piece of knowledge, a new understanding you have read about in this chapter.

14 Is it Sexy?

How to put life-force into your words

Sexy is the buzzword in television newsrooms. News stories and film-clips flood in all the time and editors have to make last-minute decisions about what to put into the newscast. As they weigh one item against another, this is the question they ask: 'Is it *sexy*?' Does it fire the imagination, shock, amuse and break away from what the composer Michael Tippett calls 'the frightened hand of mediocrity'? '*Is it sexy?*' means 'Does it have *life-force*?' – the mysterious dynamism that makes us climb mountains, go out and sell, write books, or at least get out of bed in the morning.

One research organisation has gone through contortions to come up with the finding that the attention of people in cities is momentarily caught by over 2,000 advertising messages *each day*. Add to that the thousands of other impressions made on us from morning to night. Now add all those random thoughts flitting in and out, the anxieties, doubts, terrors and confusions churning around inside us. When you are communicating with someone, all that lot is the competition!

What can you do about it? How can you really get through to people? *Ideas* are the quintessential skill in communication: this is the skill that cuts through apathy and preoccupation, that lifts your letter, advertisement, report, fax or something you say out of everyday routine and makes people react and respond. Of course some people are better at coming up with ideas than others and you may not feel you're one of those.

But you have untapped reserves of creativity. How do you get at them? You push harder, you go on pushing for longer, and you don't settle for the commonplace. We cannot deny that talent comes into it but one of the things about creative people is they work harder and longer at producing ideas. Don't stop too soon – the idea of a lifetime may be just around the corner.

Charles Saatchi, said to be the most brilliant creative advertising man of his generation, never stopped looking for a sharper cutting edge; even if a client loved an advertisement, Charles Saatchi would not hesitate to try to do something better. David Ogilvy, another legendary adman, said 'I'm terrified of producing a lousy advertisement – this causes me to throw away the first twenty attempts'. Let yourself be terrified of writing a dull letter, making a boring phone call, having a lack-lustre meeting, or sending off a tedious report. If ideas aren't flowing, stop for a few minutes and look through a magazine with a lot of pictures in it. When you stimulate and excite your brain it rewards you with more creative energy.

You have to have something to say – that's always the first step. But how you say it, the words you use are just as important, or people will switch off.

Words are the masters of the media world. They make and break reputations. And also fortunes. They give life or death to a new idea or a product. They are the all-powerful gods of the religion of writing.

Jacques Séguéla,
Ne dites pas à ma mère . . .

This is where work comes in: those seemingly off-the-cuff phrases that lift up our hearts and confront our senses are nearly always the result of a lot of effort. Politicians prefer to keep up the illusion that their speeches come straight from the heart, right off the chest, but most of them have paid 'wordprocessors', the best brains in the communication business hired to sweat out those inspiring, electrifying phrases, to be projected on to invisible glass prompt screens. George

Bush's glorious acceptance-speech vision of his America as an 'endless enduring dream and a thousand points of light' were the words of a top speech writer, Peggy Noonan, written and rewritten until they glowed with incandescence.

At one of the top courses on creativity, students are advised to think of this quality as 'an extra ingredient', like using spices in cooking – or the bubbles in champagne. We are urged not to overlook the obvious because so often the ingredient we are looking for is there all the time; but we take it for granted or write it off as not worth talking or writing about. Yet it may be the one thing that can add something different and special to a letter, an advertisement, a sales pitch or even a telephone call.

After all, the bubbles were present in champagne right from the start, but as an unwanted by-product of secondary fermentation, which for centuries the wine makers tried to reduce. Then (so the myth goes) a local monk, called Dom Pérignon, saw the possibilities. From then on the bubbles gave this hitherto modest white wine from the Champagne region of France star billing, a premium price and turned it into a world-wide mega-dollar product.

Remember the story of champagne and listen for the sound of corks popping when you communicate, because words have *fizz* too. In the search for this magic that lifts words off the paper into someone's heart, look for simplicity and directness *plus* a twist of the unexpected. It is a process of refinement – hitting the bull's-eye, rather than spreading the shots. There is always the temptation to hedge your bets with a there's-also-this-and-this approach, but if you want communication to be *sexy*, you have in the end to find the courage to select one simple point and stake the impact of your message on that. If it can carry with it the promise of that first sip of the first drink of the evening, you are on the right track.

Someone said the famous Chanel perfume after many years of investment in advertising, owes more to a sexy answer from Marilyn Monroe to a journalist's question. And what an answer! When she was asked what was her favourite nightdress, she replied: 'Chanel Number Five'. That was more than a spark jumping across – it was a flash of lightning!

'John Walker' is just another name but *'Johnnie Walker'* is *sexy*. And it was sexier still when they advertised their Black Label whisky with a shiny black page, nothing on it except for the empty life-size outline in gold of the label. Across it were the words:

> 12 years ago we put down some Scotch for you.
> Hopefully you can afford it by now.

It's not easy to make *The Economist* sexy, as it's a heavyweight financial journal, founded in 1843. But someone had an idea that succeeded. This also took up a whole page in a newspaper – in solid red type (perhaps as a warning) across the centre, were just eleven words:

> If your assistant
> reads
> *The Economist,*
> don't play
> too much golf.

Gatwick airport, twenty-seven miles south of London, became sexy when the non-stop train service direct from Victoria Station was advertised with *one word* in the centre of a big poster:

> GATQUICK!

Raymond Chandler told Ian Fleming about the most sexy book title he had ever seen:

> The Shivering Chorus Girls

There's nothing new in using words to give life-force to an idea. Words have always been able to work magic. This observation carved on an Egyptian pyramid more than 5,000 years ago still has drama in the 1990s:

> Man lives on one quarter of what he eats. On the other
> three-quarters, his doctor lives.

Those examples of sexy communication, dating from

the 1990s to 5,000BC, have the same three ingredients:

(i) The words are short and there are few of them.

(ii) They hang on one simple idea which connects immediately.

(iii) There's a hint of a double-take, a twist of the unexpected that jolts our attention.

Test our your own communication, the way you begin it, or the last sentence you write or say, against those three points. If you can tick off each one of them, you've arrived.

When you communicate with someone, it's like playing on a marvellous concert grand. You could play a little tune with one finger, using only three notes. But what a waste that would be, because there is great music in that piano, that could move and excite us. Think of every important communication in that way: is it a one-finger exercise, or are you truly exploring all the possibilities?

A mixture of insight, magic and drama is the ultimate communication skill. There are other vital prescriptions in this book you are reading that will lead to success when you have to get a message across. Here comes the final prescription, the one that adds dynamic power to all the others: look at the draft of the letter you're going to send, the report you're working on, something you're planning to say, or even a fax you've written out, and ask . . . *Is it sexy? . . . Does it have life-force? . . . Can you hear corks popping? . . . Can you put it on a T-shirt?*

REVIEW OF COMMUNICATION SKILLS

1. *Ideas* are the communication skill that cuts through apathy and preoccupation, that lifts your letter, advertisement, report, fax or something you say, out of everyday routine and makes people react and respond.

2. You can contact your untapped reserves of creativity by pushing harder and pushing for longer. Don't settle

for the commonplace. Those seemingly off-the-cuff brilliant words you read and hear are nearly always the result of a lot of work.

3. This is the ultimate communication skill: look at the draft of a letter you're going to send, a report you're working on, something you're planning to say, or even a fax you've written out, and ask . . . *Is it sexy? . . . Does it have life-force? . . . Can you hear corks popping? . . . Can you put it on a T-shirt?*

Acknowledgements

This book owes so much to many people who have contributed ideas, advice and luminous examples. I am grateful to the following and thank them also on behalf of every reader who has been helped to communicate more successfully:

Douglas Adams, *The Hitch-hiker's Guide to the Galaxy* (Pan Books, London)
Apple Macintosh, California
Audi cars
Jane Barkey, account supervisor with Ogilvy & Mather, London
David Bernstein, creative consultant, for the story about Oscar Hammerstein and Jerome Kern
Mike Bett, vice-chairman of British Telecom
Maeve Binchy, novelist, writing in *The Listener*
Rabbi Lionel Blue, for wry insights into the communication process
Lesley Bremness, for advice on using dried lavender to cure telephone tension
British Telecom
British Telecom Museum, Oxford (E T Birch, curator)
Peter Brook, *The Shifting Point* (Methuen, London)
Roy Brooks Estate Agents (A R Halstead, for permission to quote classic Roy Brooks advertisements)
Helen Gurley Brown, *Having It All* (Simon and Schuster, New York)
The late Raymond Chandler
Chartsearch, London, for their well-constructed letter about an investment system
Susannah Clapp, assistant editor of *London Review of Books*
Michael Cockerell, *Live from Number 10* (Faber, London)
Peter J Congdon, director of Gifted Children's Information Centre
Cary L Cooper, president of the British Academy of Management
Sir John Cuckney, *Advice From The Top* (David & Charles, Newton Abbot)
Marion Devine, for information about neurolinguistic programming in *The Sunday Times*

Dr Jack Dominian, psychiatrist, Central Middlesex Hospital, London
Eagle Star Insurance
Roger Eglin, business editor of *The Sunday Times*
Ivan Fallon, *The Brothers* (Century Hutchinson, London)
Dr Lesley Fallowfield, lecturer in health psychology at the London Hospital Medical College
Anna Ford, *Men* (Weidenfeld & Nicolson, London)
Richard Francis, director-general of the British Council
Dr Willard Gaylin, *Rediscovering Love* (Viking Penguin, New York)
Sir John Gielgud, for observations on the *creative pause*
Liz Gill, for information about doctors and patients (from her article in *The Sunday Times*)
Glavcosmos, the Soviet Space Administration
Kevin Goldfarb, partner with Rayner Essex, accountants
The Green Party
Stephen Greenblatt, *London Review of Books*
Roger Hancock, director of Plastics, Fabrication and Printing, Milton Keynes
Professor Charles Handy, visiting professor at the London Business School
The Hanson Group, London
Dr Sophia Hartland, psychiatrist for advice on communication between women and men
Professor Stephen W Hawking, *A Brief History of Time* (Bantam Press, London)
Sir John Harvey-Jones, *Making It Happen* (Collins, London)
Health Education Authority
Hitachi electric shavers
David Hockney, artist
John Holmes, chairman of Holmes & Marchant
Alastair Horne, biographer of Harold Macmillan (Macmillan, London)
Lee Iaocca, quoted in *The Sunday Times*
Institut Européan d'Administration des Affaires, Fontainebleau
Carl Gustav Jung, psychiatrist and luminary
Sir Hector Laing, *Advice From The Top* (David & Charles, Newton Abbot)
Dr Sammy Last, psychiatrist
Françoise Legrand, for support, encouragement and so much legwork
Fanny Leonora, for revealing new possibilities of communication between women and men
Alicja Lesniak, financial director of J Walter Thompson, London
Theodore Levitt of the Harvard Business School

Kay Lily, teacher of assertiveness at the City of London University
Terry Lunn, personnel director, Joseph Tetley & Son
The late Dr Dermod MacCarthy, paediatrician
Paul Massey, vice-president of the Institute of Personnel Management
Dudley Masters, director of UK Training, for comment on neurolinguistic programming
John May, international lecturer on communication and an inspired teacher
Dr Brian McAvoy, senior lecturer in general medical practice at Leicester University
Donald McCullin, *Is Anyone Taking Any Notice?* (MIT Press, Cambridge, Massachusetts)
Victoria McKee, *The Sunday Times*
Dr David Mendel, *Proper Doctoring* (Springer-Verlag, New York)
Masanori Moritani, *Japanese Technology* (Crown Publishers, New York)
Desmond Morris, *Manwatching* and *Bodywatching* (Jonathan Cape, London)
Penny Morris, teaching fellow in communication skills at Cambridge University
David Ogilvy, *The Unpublished David Ogilvy* (Sidgwick & Jackson, London, and Crown Publishers Inc, New York)
Ogilvy & Mather, London, advertising agency
Sir Anthony Parsons, former British ambassador to the UN
Dr David Pendleton, editor of *Doctor-Patient Communication*
Tom Peters, *Thriving on Chaos* (Alfred A Knopf, New York and Macmillan, London)
Professor Nigel Piercy and Neil Morgan of the Cardiff Business School
Dennis Potter, playwright, in *The Listener*
The Presentation Company, London, who never get slides back to tnorf
Sir Randolph Quirk, president of the British Academy
Linda Romero, pa to chief executive of BP Chemicals
Saatchi & Saatchi, advertising agency, and Charles and Maurice Saatchi
Esther Salaman, *Unlocking Your Voice* (Gollancz, London)
Kate Saunders, *The Sunday Times*
Jacques Séguéla, *Ne dites pas à ma mère que je suis dans la publicité . . . Elle me croit pianiste dans un bordel* and *Hollywood lave plus blanc* (Flammarion, Paris)
Godfrey Smith, for reminders of compelling openings to novels
Alexander Solzhenitsyn
Martin Sorrell, chairman of the WPP communications group

The Sperry Corporation, Cobham, England
David St John Thomas, former chairman of David & Charles, publishers, for starting the whole thing off with breakfast at The Savoy, London
Peter Stringfellow, nightclub owner, New York, Miami and London
Studs Terkel, *Working* (Avon Books, New York)
Margaret Thatcher
Sir Michael Tippett, *Moving into Aquarius* (Routledge & Kegan Paul, London)
Volkswagen cars
William Walton, one of the founders of Holiday Inns, writing in *Healthy Companies*
James Watson, biologist and Nobel prizewinner
Dr David Weeks, neuropsychologist at The Royal Edinburgh Hospital
Mary Wesley, novelist, writing in *The Listener*

Where appropriate, every effort has been made to acknowledge copyright holders and if there are any omissions or inaccuracies, please accept my apologies.

GH

Index

Italic numbers indicate quotations